GAYDAR

"Hmmm, he must be. I mean, look at his haircut
and shirt (any tighter, and he wouldn't be able to breathe)
—and, oh my God! that butt!
Besides, isn't he staring right at me?!"

GAYDAR

THE ULTIMATE INSIDER GUIDE TO THE GAY SIXTH SENSE

DONALD F. REUTER

Crown Publishers
NEW YORK

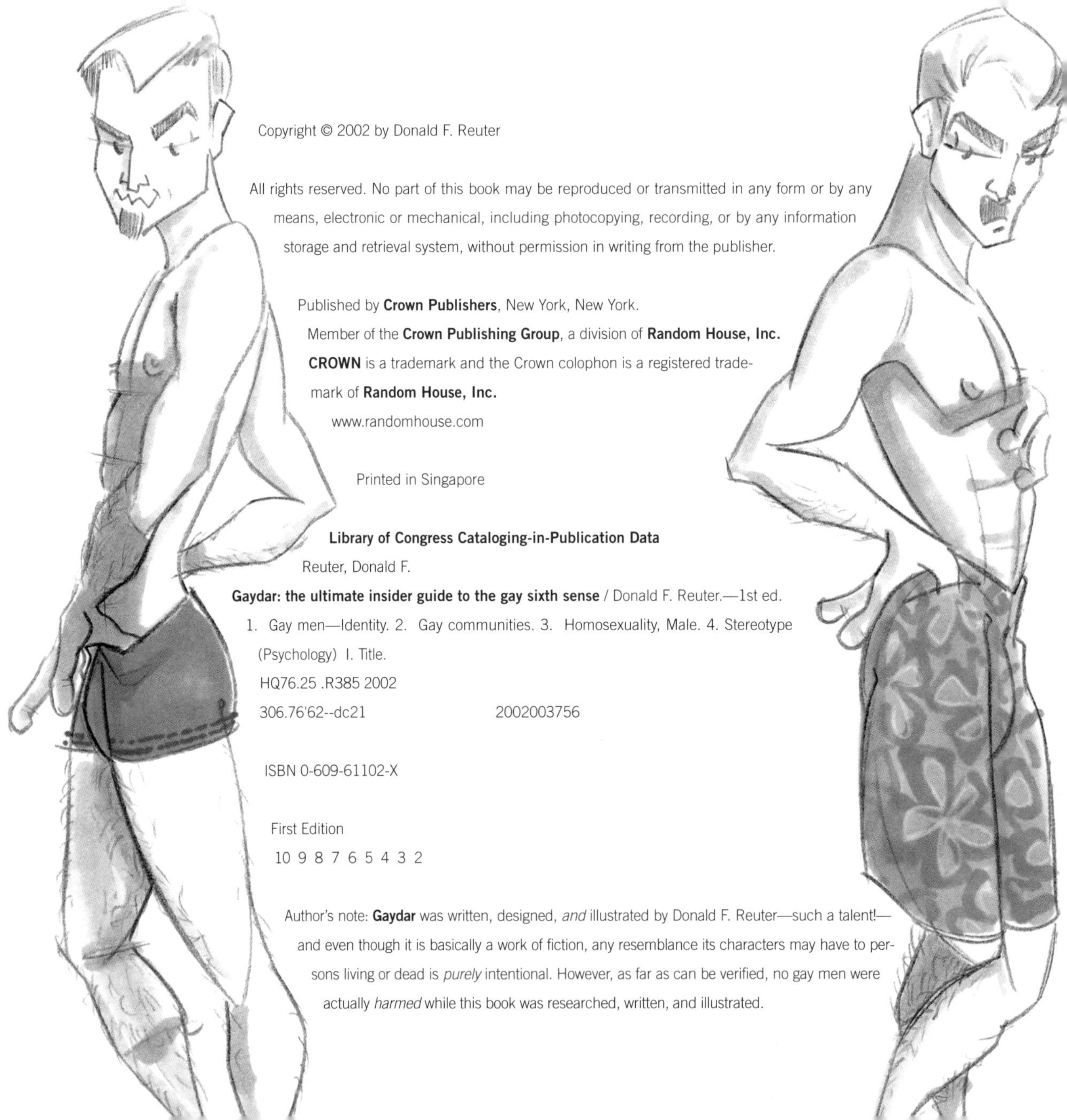

Published by **Crown Publishers**, New York, New York.
Member of the **Crown Publishing Group**, a division of **Random House, Inc.**
CROWN is a trademark and the Crown colophon is a registered trademark of **Random House, Inc.**
www.randomhouse.com

Printed in Singapore

Library of Congress Cataloging-in-Publication Data
Reuter, Donald F.
Gaydar: the ultimate insider guide to the gay sixth sense / Donald F. Reuter.—1st ed.
1. Gay men—Identity. 2. Gay communities. 3. Homosexuality, Male. 4. Stereotype (Psychology) I. Title.
HQ76.25 .R385 2002
306.76'62--dc21 2002003756

ISBN 0-609-61102-X

First Edition
10 9 8 7 6 5 4 3 2

Author's note: **Gaydar** was written, designed, *and* illustrated by Donald F. Reuter—such a talent!—and even though it is basically a work of fiction, any resemblance its characters may have to persons living or dead is *purely* intentional. However, as far as can be verified, no gay men were actually *harmed* while this book was researched, written, and illustrated.

to those who can laugh first at themselves—before laughing at others—*Gaydar *is dedicated

The author would also like to gratefully acknowledge the contributions of the following people, without whom *Gaydar* would never have come to pass: my "open-minded" editor, Doug Pepper, Mark McCauslin, Derek McNally, Thaddeus Bower, Jennifer O'Connor, and all at **Crown** who lent a helping hand; my agent, the indominitable Caroline Sparrow; all my family, friends (and foes); Red (of course); and most especially to Robert, for acceptance of my "gayness" and the welcome display of his own.

gaylist

THE "ULTIMATE" GUIDE?

Sure, and why not?! I felt that my *humble* Midwestern upbringing, *exotic* Eurasian ethnicity, coming out in my impressionable mid-teens, decades-long work in the fields of fashion, beauty, and publishing in the center of it all, New York City, coupled with years of in-depth (and I mean *deep*) research gave me undisputable qualifications to speak as a *gay*-thority on the subject. The modest realization of this fact and the importance of you needing to know from an "expert" was all the excuse I needed to take pen and paper in hand and open my big ol' mouth. Besides, it wasn't as though I needed permission from an authorized committee of gay men (ever try to get a group of us to unanimously decide in favor of anything?). So get ready, *girls,* the "cat" is being let out of the bag—and its claws are "jungle red." (Which is part of a line read by what actress in what film? See page 132.)

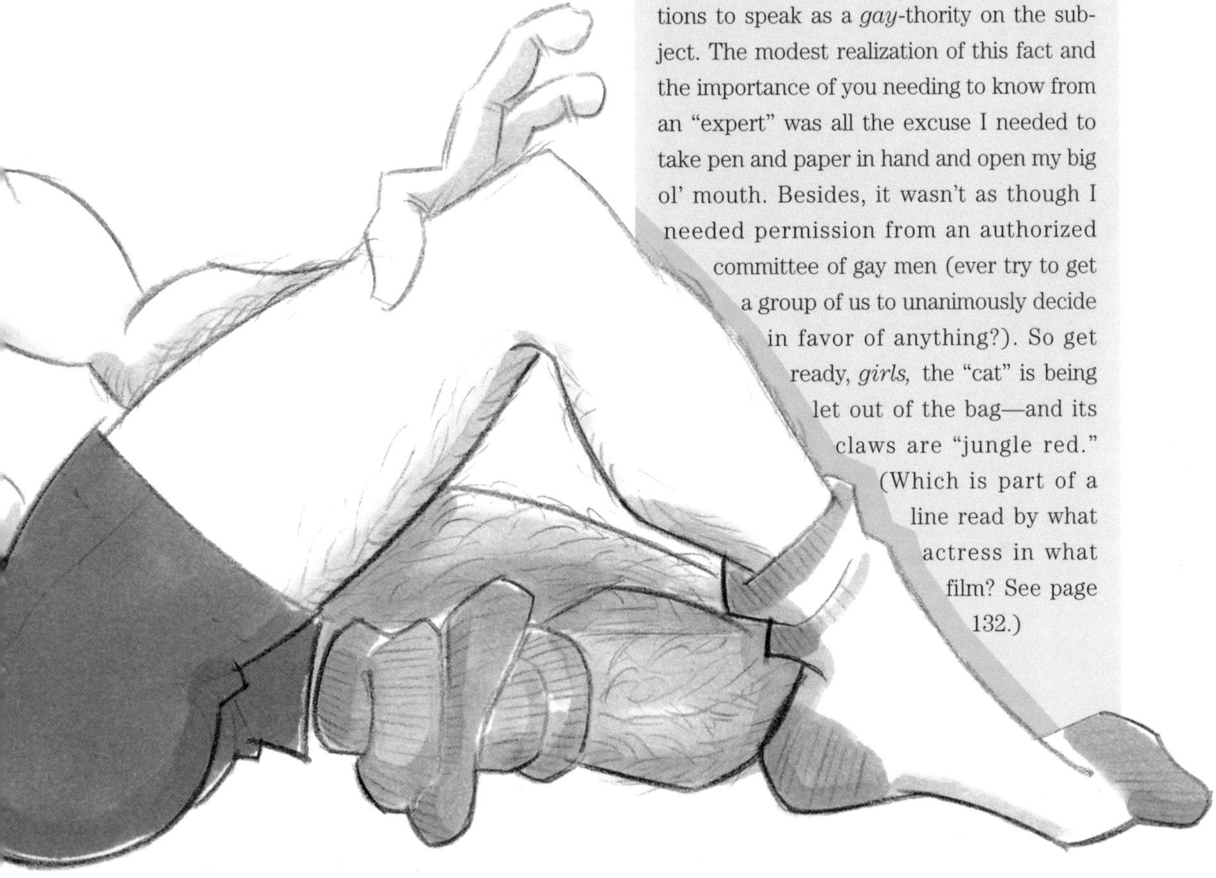

Welcome, friends and "friends I have yet to know."*

Many are familiar with the term *gaydar*, but not exactly sure what it means. Simply, it is a word (derived from radar, of course) used to name the telepathic sixth sense which only gay men—and the occasional *ultra* savvy straight person—seem to possess. Its main function is to help gay men recognize one another in situations involving the general straight population (hockey games, Denny's, et al). But in addition, *gaydar* can used to determine leading fashion, music, film, and decorating trends. This makes it a very handy tool to have at your beck and call (if knowing such things is important, which is often the case with gay men).

However, as gays flow into the mainstream and continue to assimilate its mental and physical characteristics—both good *and* bad—many feel we have become difficult to spot within the larger group (which does make being gay sound a little James Bond-ish). This has made understanding how *gaydar* works an even more pressing matter. Nevertheless, it is not true that today's gay man (is that a clothing store?!) is any more difficult to uncover than he was in the past. In days gone by, with the great majority of gay men "in the closet"—by no choice of their own—it was definitely harder to keep an accurate homosexual head count. Nowadays, many still choose to be invisible by wearing the "suit" or a "beard" (an old term used to describe a woman seen in the company of a closeted gay man), but enough visible fairies are out sprinkling pixie dust in the faces of the uncomfortable to make us seem like we are *everywhere*—and we definitely are. Further, many gay men like to keep their distance away from the masses in a self-created realm difficult to copy by straight people (and other gay men) and will up the ante of exclusivity. Regardless, no matter how fondly gays may be embraced by the heterosexual community—leaving our former estrangement as a sad reminder of what used to be—*gaydar* remains a necessary device for those thousands (maybe millions) of hapless gay men and unwary straight women to avoid such embarrassing revelatory moments as, "Oh, I thought you were . . . ," "Oh, I didn't know you were . . . ," and the ever-popular "But isn't he married?!," and so forth.

* This quote is from a "gay-fave" film. If you know which one—and who *sang* it—you *probably* don't need *Gaydar.* If you haven't a clue, this is right place for the answer (see page 132).

WARNING!

Gaydar (the book) is assembled around the exploits of literally and figuratively idealized gay males whom many will no doubt view as—*argh! don't say it!*—stereotypes. However, whilst some of you cringe at the thought, because gay men actually do come in such an infinite range of shapes, sizes, colors, and dispositions, it was necessary to select this *limited* range in order to focus the book. (Regrettably, it was also not possible to include any of the nuances of lesbian *gaydar,* itself a science far from the complete understanding of most gay men and deserving of its own book.) Constructing *Gaydar* this way is really no different than a cable station being marketed as "women's television" (meaning only *they* can watch?!), or another excusing its contents as a "guy thing" (does that include gay guys?!). My reasoning may not make *Gaydar* any more acceptable to the politically correct diehard, but my intention was not to demean anyone. For what it's worth, I humbly offer this simple sentiment:

Gay men do not all behave, look, act, or think like the "men" presented in *Gaydar*—even though they are, by and large, a *marvelously* sexy, witty, wise, and frequently hunky group. (I know I may have to remind you of this from time to time.)

WARNING, TOO!

Further on the subject of this book, as the *très* gay, "mature" (don't ask, it's not polite), mincing (but still leanly muscled) author, I have based *Gaydar's* contents largely on my own personal actions, behavior, and experiences. However, I expect many people—especially within the gay community—to take umbrage at my saying that anyone *else's* actions, behavior, or experiences can be unequivocably construed as being "gay" or "straight." In reality, I do not make this claim. But one must accept at the core of each instance brought up in *Gaydar* there is some truth, otherwise it would not have been included. As long as there are those (gay men among them) who consider being gay a negative thing, presentations of "gayness"—in books like *Gaydar*—will continue to ruffle feathers. (Would there be the same stigma if the word "gay" had the same connotations as "honorable" or "kind"?) When the time finally arrives where gay men (and women) are unconditionally accepted and championed *Gaydar* will become little more than a dated book filled with quaint sentiment and questionable humor. In the meantime, here is yet another necessary caveat:

You could be the most fun to be around, fabulously dressed, best dancing, thin and muscular, neatly groomed, great-in-bed, sensitive man in the world and still be straight as an arrow; on the flipside, you can watch football, hook worms and fish, spit on the sidewalk, shoot Bambi's mother, scratch your ass in public, and still be gay-as-the-month-of-May. (Honestly, I don't see how any of this is possible, but they tell me you're both out there somewhere.)

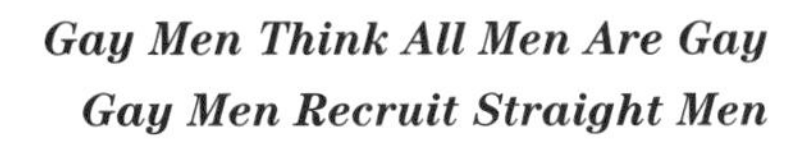

Gay Men Think All Men Are Gay
Gay Men Recruit Straight Men

First, most gay men do not subscribe to either of these blanket theories. Second, at least ten percent of the total male population—straight *and* gay—are so completely self-centered, uncaring, and moronic, no one wants to take credit for them. Third, no man can truthfully claim to be one hundred percent gay *or* straight (without crossing fingers behind his back).

Personally, while I consider myself to be so gay there should be a new word for it—and proud of it—there are a few aspects of my personality which I cannot attribute to anything other than straight male in origin. To wit, this "dude" likes to shovel in his food when eating; occasionally pee in the shower (admittedly, an economic use of time); and, most brazenly, likes to adjust his "privates" in public. I know there are many heterosexual male traits not as offensive, but I do think I made my point. Conversely, straight men should allow that they will have some gay aspect(s) to their personalities—and not just the libidinous clichés that come to mind.

Does *Gaydar* have an agenda? Yes, but only to make it clear that nothing involving the human condition is finite. Meanings for "straight," "gay," "masculine," and "feminine" are changing, merging, even disappearing. Straight or gay, any man reading through *Gaydar* will find attributes of his own personality—*beyond the obsession with his phallus!*—which may give him pause. But it could be one that refreshes.

GAYDO AND GAYDONT

A long, *long* time ago—*way* before I was born, doll!—*gaydar* began as a series of secret "signals" used by unacknowledged gay men to search for one another in a rather unaccepting and at times hostile straight environment. They ranged from the subtle gesture—wearing a red tie—to the blatantly overt—calling acquaintances by feminine names, "sister," "Mary," and "girlfriend" (my, my, times haven't changed much over the years, have they?!), and *Gaydar* contains many of these "signs" that have become classics.* In the meantime, to help you get more acquainted with the subject, here are some basic primers which every gay man takes with him—figuratively—when he is out scanning with his own *gaydar*.

The Only Surefire Way to Know

Unhesitating admittal to being gay, with the understanding that when sex takes place it is exclusively with men. (Did you think this was going to be something else?!) Too-frequent homosexual "experimentation" is also highly suspect.

The Anti-Gay

Any man who acts *too* straight—which includes the vehement denial of *any* gay tendencies to the expression of violent anti-gay feelings—is someone who may be desperately overcompensating for something about himself that he is afraid to admit and accept. This *ungentle,* overtly "manly" man warrants exceptionally close scrutiny.

Hiding in Plain Sight

Not surprisingly, you may find the above man "hiding" in an unquestionably heterosexual stronghold: the military, fraternity houses, men's clubs, and so on. (The church can also be listed here, but its internal *man*-ifestations stem from entirely different circumstances and lead to their own special set of consequences.) Just below the surface all these places are rife with homo-friendly behavior, ranging from the minor teasing skirmishes to full-on, no-holds-barred, man-to-man, sexual activities. This all may be news to them, but is it really news to you?!

*To help you find "*gaydar* classics" in this book, they will be designated as such and printed in color for easy recognition.

Numbers Don't Lie

One or two instances of "gay" behavior does not a fairy make. However, once you go over everything, things can start to add up quickly. You will find a great many "straight" men are just a hop, skip, and a jump away from taking a full time share—with all the perks—in Candyland. (Note: There is a "gay" questionnaire at the end of this book for you to try and keep an accurate accounting of your friends and acquaintances.)

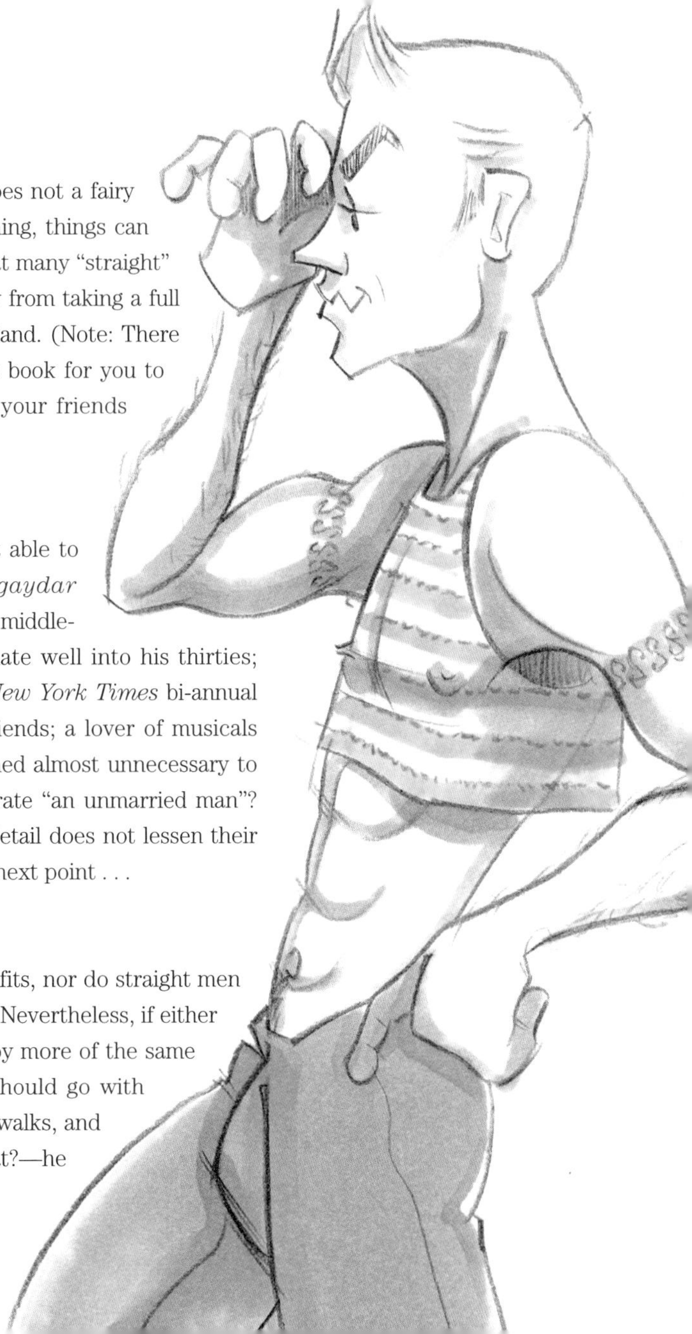

An Oldie but a Goodie

Since space is limited in *Gaydar*, I'm not able to include everything. Fortunately, some *gaydar* things were *so* obvious—the good-looking, middle-aged, *unmarried* man; having a roommate well into his thirties; reads fashion magazines (including *The New York Times* bi-annual style editions); lots of platonic female friends; a lover of musicals *and* gladiator movies, and so on—it seemed almost unnecessary to mention them. Besides, ever try to illustrate "an unmarried man"? However, leaving them out from further detail does not lessen their potential accuracy. Which leads me to my next point . . .

A Rose Is a Rose

Gay men do not own the market on hissy fits, nor do straight men possess all the shares in boorish manners. Nevertheless, if either behaves in such a manner, compounded by more of the same obvious sexually oriented actions, you should go with your gut instincts: if he looks, acts, talks, walks, and even smells gay (or straight)—guess what?—he probably is. Not that it should matter!

INTRODUCING, MISS CONCEPTION!

Now, to somewhat contradict what you've just read, a friend of mine, "Miss Conception" (I know, *you clever minxes*, the Cher wig gives her away), would like to go over some things first. Since time immemorial, false assumptions have beset the gay community, and though many have a basis in reality—and *Gaydar* includes quite a few—"Connie" wishes to make it perfectly clear, *darling readers*, that all gay men are not:

flamers

While there is absolutely nothing wrong with being a screaming, nelly, swishy queer—someone who, I might add, can be a great person to be around and highly entertaining company—most gay men behave just like the vast majority of average folk. Okay, we're a touch more sensitive in general, and tend to obsess over silly things, but still pretty dull.

drag queens

Gads, *honey*, are you kidding?! First, most of us look upon wearing women's clothes with about as much enthusiasm as having teeth removed. Second, being gay does not automatically mean you are any good at it; most would end up looking like James Gandolfini in a gown—not a pretty picture. However, when we do it well, *sister,* nobody does it better.

promiscuous

The belief is that all gay men act like walking erections (but hey, don't *all* men?!). In truth, we only have a less restrictive attitude toward sex, but even that does not mean we can be found in as many hotel bedrooms as the Gideon Bible. Many may find this hard to believe, but more gay men are serious about *monogamy*—which is not the name of a board game—than are not. (Incidentally, neither course of action is the more correct way to practice sexuality.)

bitchy, bitter, and jaded

Admittedly, we have an abundance of these three graceless graces—and all of us have our little tirades—but they don't come close to outnumbering the millions of nice, "normal," and not-so-jaded men who wouldn't know the difference between a barb and a Barbie doll. The same sentiment goes for expecting us all to be anal, arrogant, and pretentious.

gallant and well-mannered

Gay men will be the first to let you enter or exit the elevator or doorway, and always extend a "please," "excuse me," and "thank you" for even the most trifling interactions. But, *honey-buns,* if we're running late—especially for the theatre or a sex date with a hot hunk—it's every man, woman, child, and *queen* for themselves.

stylish, creative, and in-the-know

Just because our "brothers" include Bernstein and Beaton, Cukor and Coward, Dior and Diaghelev, doesn't mean we are all automatically accepted into the gay fraternity "house of style." It takes an initiation, and not every pledge makes the cut. As far as knowing all about current trends in fashion, film, and so forth, while many gay men do stay one step ahead of the pack in that regard, most consider standing on the cutting edge to be a little too sharp.

neat, clean, and organized

A hallmark of a gay man is impeccable personal cleanliness, but his hygienic ways don't always extend homeward. Some of our houses are so dirty the only thing distinguishing the spaces from the outside are the walls, and the only signs of "culture" are growing in the refrigerator (hyuck! hyuck!). But seriously folks, being gay does not instantly make you Mr Clean (although someone in their advertising department obviously visited a few gay bars to conjur such a homo-erotic hottie), or as ordered as a walking Filofax.

Pardon, *dear hearts*, but these next three are a little on the serious side:

more accepting of differences

We extol the virtues of a "rainbow tribe," but, sadly, still have reservations when it comes to total acceptance of others—especially within our own community. Too often we are huddled in infamous and exclusionary gay *cliques,* where you will find the prudish pilloring the promiscuous, musclemen muscling out the skinny, and one ethnic group avoiding another.

a straight woman's best friends

From the first moment we were spotted "hanging out with the girls," gay men have been joined at the hip with straight women. But hairline fissures make this a fragile conjoining at best. Many straight women expect gay friends to be sensitive and understanding, stylish and witty. If not, there are plenty of unsophisticated straight men to occupy their time. For our part, many gay men perpetuate the ultra-feminine "pretty woman" ideal, mainly through our work, which, among other things, allows us to appear more masculine by comparison.

more feminine than masculine-acting

The general population believes that acting "gay" is an inherently feminine mode of behavior, and no way for a "man" to be. This implies that "feminine" traits are less preferable than "masculine" ones. Still with me, *hon?* Unfortunately, there are plenty of gay men who believe this and consider it an obligation to act like "men" in order to be accepted. Ponder this: Is the "feminine"-behaving straight man better or worse than the "masculine"-acting gay guy?

This frequently gay-supported notion also suffers upon close inspection:

"friend of Dorothy"

There was a time when you could assume a fan of Judy Garland (aka Dorothy in *The Wizard of Oz*) was going to be gay. That's still a safe bet, but times change and so does the *diva du jour.* Some time ago, Madonna *replaced* "Judy" for many younger generation gay men. Eventually, Ms Ciccione, too, will be supplanted by another fabulous *femme fatale.* Applications are now being accepted.

Finally, the last misconception (yippee!). It also happens to be the one trap that gay men have set for themselves. That being the existence of the:

poofdah resistance

On the one hand, "he" can be a wonderful gay role model: intelligent, witty, attractive, athletic, and thoughtful—someone *every* man should aspire to be like. On the other hand, many of his kind have metamorphosed into almost other-worldly beings of superior intellect, acerbic humor, too conscious of their looks, how they live, and who think only of themselves. This A-list (is there even a B-list?) *gay*-titude came about purely by way of appreciable circumstances. We were entitled to our time in the spotlight after years of standing in the shadow of straight people. However, Mr Perfect's self-conscious manner makes most "other" gay men feel insecure about who they are, what they've accomplished, and where they will go in life. Take heart in knowing that this *crème de la queer* truly exists only by the handful—and they dislike each other as much as we tolerate them.

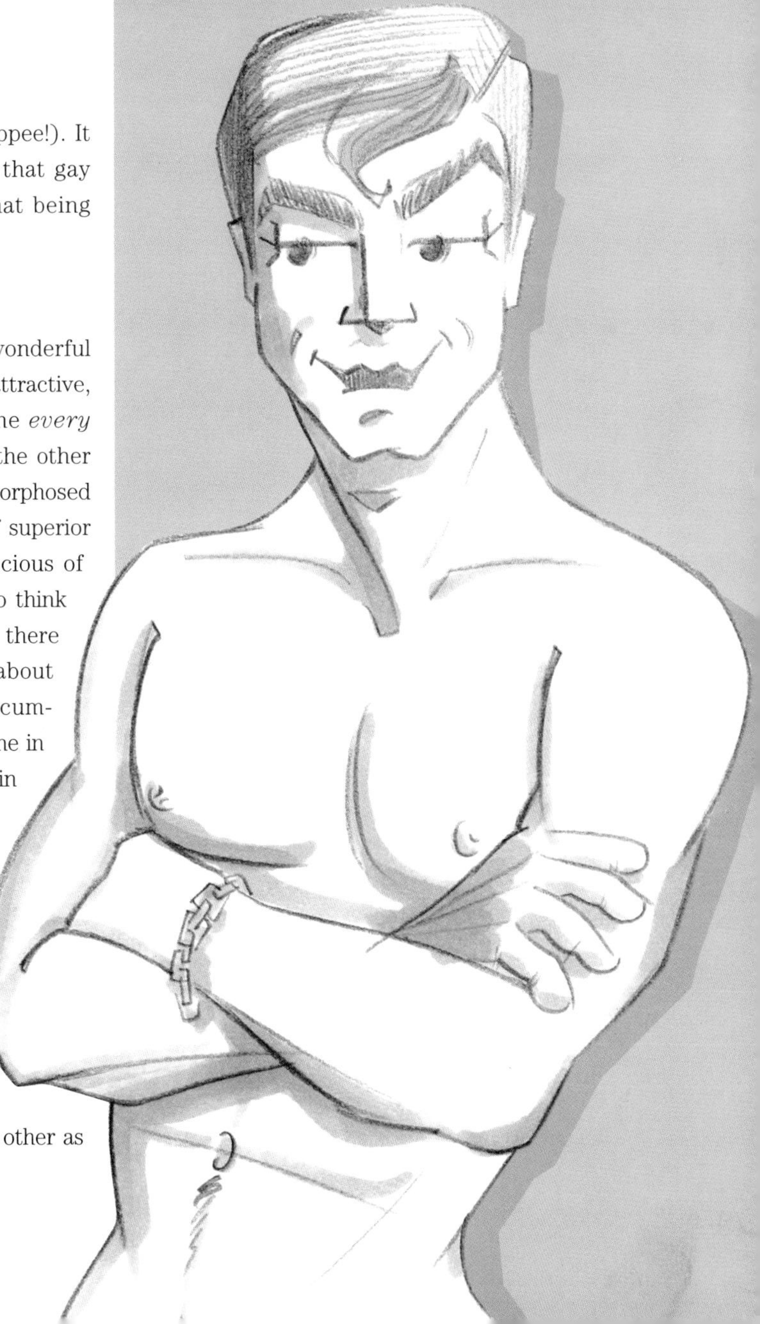

THE THREE PHASES OF STEVE

Whoa, Sherlock! Here is one more reason why sleuthing about for gay men using *gaydar* may not be as easy as dusting for fingerprints on a bottle of lubricant. (Groan.) At any one given moment, the man in question may still be caught up in "The Three Phases of Steve" (which is a wordplay on what movie title? see page 132):

denial phase - still-in-the-closet-née-straight
overcompensation phase - aggressively gay
reality phase - acceptance-of-who-he-is-and-not-really-a-phase-at-all

Therefore, his true gay self is still a work in progress. In phase one, "Steve" is still making himself invisible to spying eyes; in phase two, he is usually running in the opposite direction of anonymity, with a "smoking gun" in hand (*naughty boy*, and here so easy to catch!); in phase three, our man may just run up to you with a full confession, but is guilty of nothing more than just being himself. Amongst these three there are also many sub-phases—which *all* could end up as the final "reality" phase. "Who am I?! What am I?!" (Name the character, actress, and film! See page 132.) A selection:

drag - it may be momentary, but every gay man has been here at least once
Charles Atlas - becomes a "muscle boy" in reaction to having "sand" kicked in his face
militant - where he dares you to anger him with an anti-gay slur or gesture
wallflower - not in denial, but definitely not "out" in front
wanton - when he discovers the "candy store" of gay sex
do-gooder - trying hard to prove he is a good boy to everyone
attitude - as in, better than everyone else, including other gay men
pride - flag carrying and button wearing, but not as in-your-face as the "militant"
jaded - upon discovering that life is not a bowl of maraschino cherries

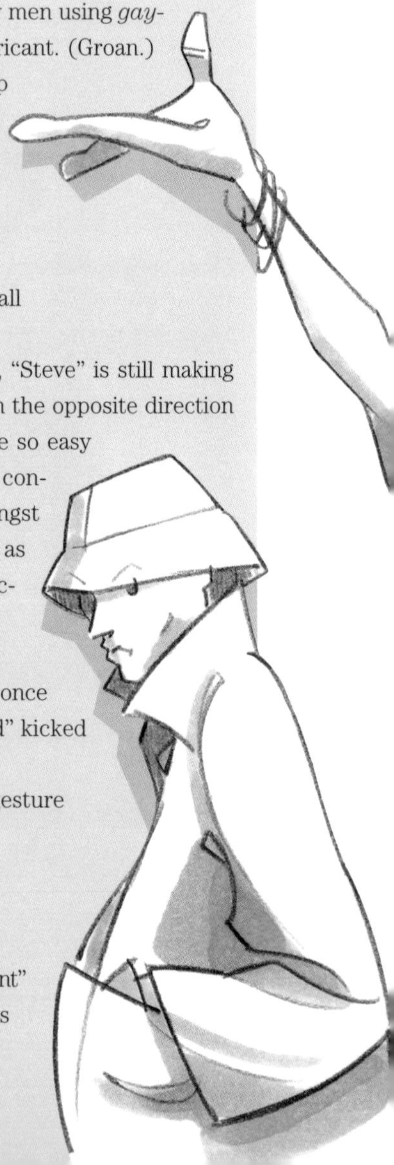

GAYDAR 2 GO!

In *Gaydar*, read *"between the lines"* this one consistent thought: *these are things gay men will (might) do and straight men will (might) not.* This way, I don't have to keep repeating myself. At the end of the book, remember I have also included a summary questionnaire for those wanting to go that extra step and start their own gay census. But keep in mind a couple things before breaking open the gay Pandora's box full of trouble: *gaydar* is not a policing tool and being gay is not a crime (at least not in most states!). Nor is it prudent to assume the techniques discussed herein have the absolute power to find *every* gay person on the planet—if they were, I'd be very rich! *There are no absolutes where people are concerned.* However, one thing is for sure, *sweetie,* you will never "look" at any man the same way again!

You can now begin your journey to gay discovery.

For these beginning few pages, your dial is set on gay radio. If your ear is not properly attuned, the sound may be a bit *queer* (sorry, *girls!*), especially if one is not accustomed to such high-pitched or hissing frequencies. (In fact, it may be helpful to catch the subtleties of *Gaydar* if, in your mind, you use the "voice" of Edward Everett Horton, Paul Lynde, Tony Randall, or Sean Hayes as you read though its entire contents.) However, don't think that all gay men speak with a lisp, or end sentences with a melodious upturned last syllable of the last *word*. Yes, many overdramatize speech with exaggerated details, wildly gesticulating hands, and contorted faces, but, my bridled friend, many more do not. We can shout just like truck drivers and drunken sailors—*if* we so desire. Listen and learn.

JUST FOR LAUGHS

To start, let's go with pure sounds and three distinct ways gay men laugh (with names that oddly sound like villains from *Batman*; the "camp" classic TV show, *nubbins*, not the movie).

The "Sniggerer"

Sometimes sounding like escaping air and usually accompanied by the most arrogant of facial expressions—a raised eyebrow—this laugh (if you can call it that) is the most subdued *and* stingy. It will likely originate more from sarcastic indifference than good-naturedness.

The "Giggler"

An incessant, at times annoying, laugh similar to that used by schoolgirls who have just discovered boys. (Come to think of it, gay men share a lot in common with schoolgirls!) Frequently employs the modest "teeth-hiding" hand gesture, making it look very coquettish or geisha girl (your choice) to the viewer. Also known as "The Titterer."

The "Guffawer"

This bellowing sound—a cross between dropping the A-bomb and channeling Phyllis Diller—is the most obvious and (not so unintentionally) attention-getting laugh. It can jangle even the most steely nerves of an unwary bystander. If you are in known company of one, it would serve you well to finish hot beverages before entering into conversation.

Perv

Gay men make these "special" noises, too. Which I swear, if turned up to the right decibel level, can shatter glass, set off car alarms two blocks away, and send dogs running for cover. Everyone ready with their cottonballs.

THE 5 GAY SQUEALS

It may "sound" like a singing quintet at a homo-version of Disneyland (is that redundant?) but, unfortunately, it's not. Likely, one of these eardrum-bursting tones will escape the lips of a single nervous little nelly wound so tightly his every thought is ready to burst out of his wide open mouth, *sans* warning. But you, you lucky devil, are getting ample time to prepare. The five are:

The "I Haven't Seen Ya for Ages!" Squeal

Occurs when the "squealer" comes face-to-face with the soon-to-be-near-deaf "squealee," neither having seen the other for quite some time. This most commonly takes place coming head-on around a corner, with shopping bags in tow; turning and walking away from an open bar, with drink in hand; or when the elevator doors open, and your boss is standing right next to you.

The "You Look Fa-a-abulous, Girl!" Squeal

A similar squeal to the above. However, in order for this one to occur or have any authenticity, the "squealee" must look noticeably different in appearance from when last seen by the "squealer." However, a disclaimer: you can question the motive of the squeal by assuming that the noisy assailant may not have had time to think of a more suitable expression for his horrified *inner* reaction to what he views as your obviously poor judgment in choosing a new haircut, outfit, or shoes.

The "I Love This Song" Squeal

Quite often whole groups of gay men utter this sound at the same time, which is typically followed by their mad dash to the nearest already overcrowded dance floor. This migratory pattern can resemble a stampeding but graceful herd of gazelles and be most disconcerting for anyone not accustomed to such *gay*-sational phenomenons (or the overwhelming olfactory onslaught of sweetly scented sweat). A successful attempt at the latest pop-star-style choreographed dance movements will ensue. Then another gay phenom—the ritualistic doffing of shirts—is topped off (or gone over the top) with lots of waving hands in the air and chants to show that you "just-don't-care." (Note: If the follow-up tune is not up to snuff, watch for the equally riveting "dance floor gay guy exodus.")

The "It's What I've Always Wanted" Squeal

If it is truly something he has always wanted—mind you, it better be from Tiffany's to be sure—there is no way for a gay man to fake this squeal. (You may be thinking this is the "I love it, Mom" ohhh sound. Not. That one means you actually hate it, and are anxiously awaiting the next box to unwrap.) This sound also resembles the "You Dirty Boy!" squeal which occurs when a gift is slightly to overtly pornographic (sex toys, X-rated ephemera, and the like).

The "There's a Roach, Spider, or Centipede in the Kitchen, Bedroom, or Bathroom" Squeal

This squeal is usually followed in quick succession by a "thunk" and "splat" sound—courtesy of a shoe or boot—administered by the "daddy" (see page 29) of the relationship coming to the rescue and smushing the little offending vermin dead in his tracks. The "squealer," however, may end up being the one to clean up. Ewww!

THINGS THAT MAKE HIM GO AWWWW!

We share this sound with gushy women who buy those *delightful* wooden lawn people, kitchen witches (for keeping bad cooking juju away), and hanging macramé doorknob decorations. It can be heard at:

- craft stores (which sell the above) in not too out-of-the-way highway hamlets
- card stores especially during Christmastime when you can buy a pull-on-his-string-and-the-nose-lights-up Santa pin (isn't that just *so* cute?!)
- gift shops specializing in tiny ceramic mice licking even tinier ice cream cones, or—hold on to your bunny suits, kiddies—stuffed animals dressed up as *other* stuffed animals (have you *evuh!**)
- in the kitchen of a dear male friend (or maiden aunt) who dotes on assorted vintage knickknackery, from salt-'n'-pepper shakers made to look like television sets to Technicolor cookie jars in the shape of—I'll give you a moment to think—big cookies!
- the plush "pet" department at FAO Schwarz (everyone say awwww!)
- In front of the window of a "real" pet shop

* This pronunciation comes from what gay composer and film score? See page 132.

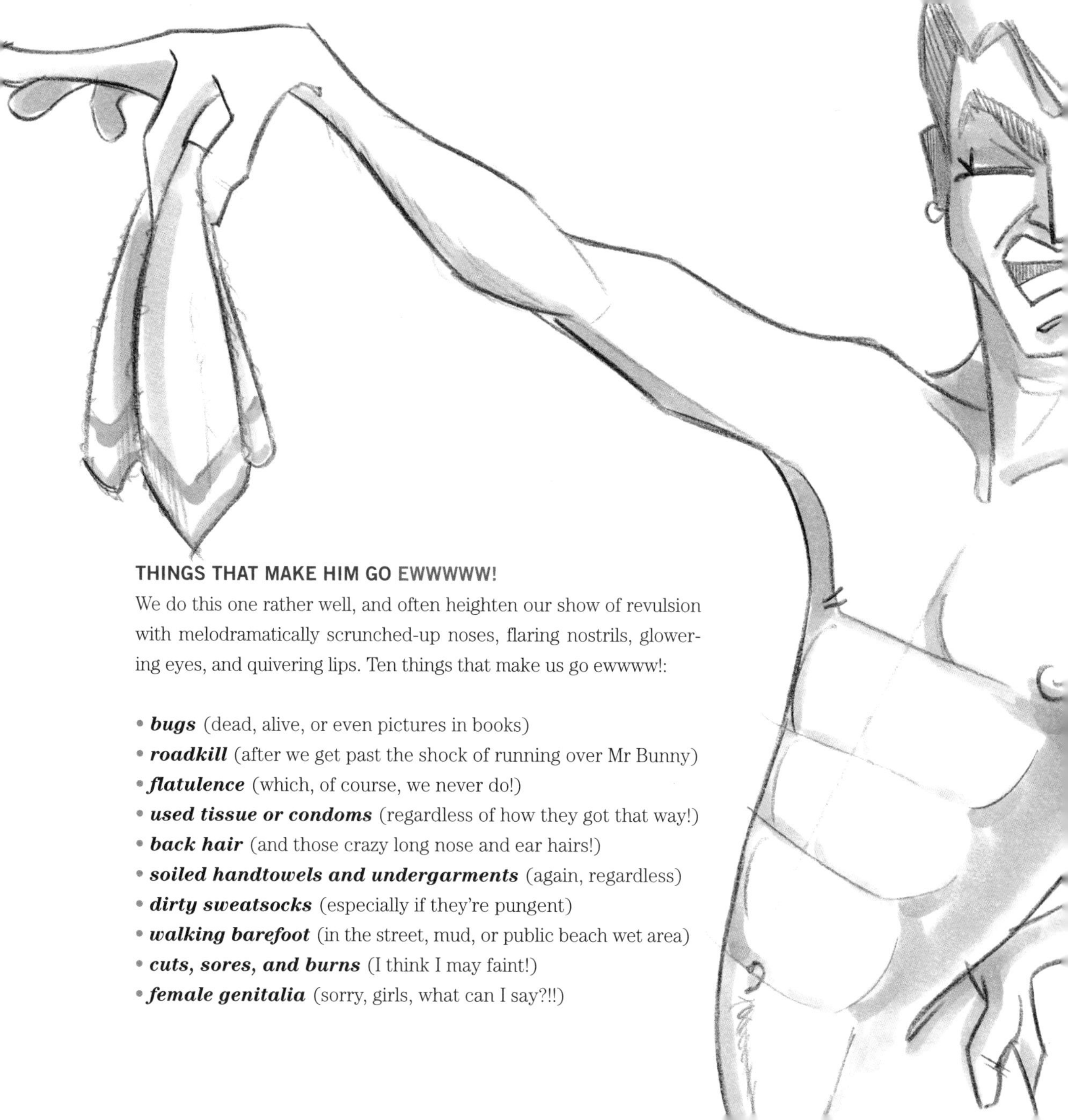

THINGS THAT MAKE HIM GO EWWWWW!

We do this one rather well, and often heighten our show of revulsion with melodramatically scrunched-up noses, flaring nostrils, glowering eyes, and quivering lips. Ten things that make us go ewwww!:

- ***bugs*** (dead, alive, or even pictures in books)
- ***roadkill*** (after we get past the shock of running over Mr Bunny)
- ***flatulence*** (which, of course, we never do!)
- ***used tissue or condoms*** (regardless of how they got that way!)
- ***back hair*** (and those crazy long nose and ear hairs!)
- ***soiled handtowels and undergarments*** (again, regardless)
- ***dirty sweatsocks*** (especially if they're pungent)
- ***walking barefoot*** (in the street, mud, or public beach wet area)
- ***cuts, sores, and burns*** (I think I may faint!)
- ***female genitalia*** (sorry, girls, what can I say?!!)

WHAT'S IN A WORD?

Now a gay language lesson. There are a number of words (possibly thousands, but who has time to count?!) which just happen to sound *gayer* than others, and can make any person who uses them sound quite gay (or "gayer" as the case may be). If you don't believe me, have *any* man use one of the words below in a complete sentence:

scintillating	**superb**	**exquisite**	**divine**	**sprinkle**
nattily	**dandy**	**delightful**	**aplomb**	**creamy**
precious	**smattering**	**smidge**	**festoon**	**enchanting**

If he hesitates, stumbles, or muffs it up completely, he's straight. Guaranteed. If the word inserts itself effortlessly into the sentence and proceeds to roll off the tongue—like 'e was 'enry 'iggins 'imself—need I say more?

The Gay Magic of O-U-S

Lucky listener, many of the "gayest" sounding words just happen to end with the letters O-U-S:

fabulous	**marvelous**	**pendulous**	**langourous**	**odiferous**
stupendous	**incredulous**	**tremulous**	**meticulous**	**vociferous**

The Gay Writing on the Wall

In a written affectation only gay men seem to indulge, many cross their "7s," "Zs," and in extreme cases "Os," presumeably to make their penmanship appear more continental. We also write "theatre" instead of "theater," and with the addition of "u" make words like "glamour" and "parlour" even more impressive. Stay alert for the use of this triage of "T"-ending words—"aught," "naught," and "fraught"—and this Anglo-ish assortment of others:

methinks	**amidst**	**amongst**	**betwixt**	**traipse**
aforementioned	**notwithstanding**	**heretofore**	**wherewithal**	**thereupon**
oft	**shan't**	**dreamt**	**spoilt**	**whilst**

THE "QUOTABLE" QUEER

Quoting movie dialogue is a habit gay men have used since the birth of the "talkie." From introductory clips—"*Willkomen, Bienvenu,* Welcome!" (*Cabaret,* 1972)—to pure camp moments—"Frankly, my dear, I don't give a damn" (*Gone With the Wind,* 1939)—lines from Tinseltown's *finest* screenplays just seem to say it all. Ten additional script snippets:

- "Fasten your seatbelts, it's going to be a bumpy night." (*All About Eve*, 1950)
- "Mr DeMille, I'm ready for my close-up." (*Sunset Boulevard*, 1950)
- "Well, Broadway doesn't go for booze and pills." (*Valley of the Dolls*, 1967)
- "Toto, I don't think we're in Kansas anymore." (*The Wizard of Oz*, 1939)
- "The world is a banquet, but most poor suckers are starving to death." (*Auntie Mame*, 1958)
- "When Steven doesn't like what I'm wearing, I take it off!" (*The Women*, 1939)
- "Hello, Gorgeous." (*Funny Girl*, 1968)
- "When you talk about this—and you will—be kind." (*Tea and Sympathy*, 1957)
- "I have always depended on the kindness of strangers." (*A Streetcar Named Desire*, 1951)
- "Well, *that's* the pot calling the kettle beige." (*The Boys in the Band*, 1970)

Gay men also have a trio of succinct sayings—along the lines of "the check is in the mail"—that come in handy for almost any situation, much to the chagrin of others:

"presentation is everything"
"it has a gay sensibility"
"the original is better"

We also have a threesome of brief but blistering statements—alterable to suit the occasion—ready to undermine the confidence of all but the most resilient recipient:

- "No, doll, that doesn't work there, it clashes with *the object you thought would work*."
- "Oh, honey, no one wears *your favorite designer* anymore!"
- "Sweetheart, nobody—and I mean nobody—has been to *your favorite spot* in ages!"

WHAT'S IN A NAME?

Like straight men who heterosexual-*ize* each other's name by adding *meister* or *man*—example: the Don-*meister*, the Don-*man*—gay men do something similar with their friend's names. Lets call it a *gay*-ification. Take for instance my name, Donald. The majority of all people have called me Don; short, not-too-sweet, and direct. However, a closer gay acquaintance may choose to *gay*-ify my name thusly:

Donald - when he is being formal with me
Donny *(or spelled Donnie)* - when feeling casual or intimate
Don-ella *(or Donalda)* - when he's feeling particularly "happy"

This is quite easy to do with a number of boy names. (What fun, huh?!) Let's try it with versions using Rob, Joe, and Frank:

Robert	***Joseph***	***Franklin***
Robbie	***Joey***	***Frankie***
Roberta	***Jo-ella*** *(or Josephine)*	***Francine***

Just for You

If your name—like Kevin or James—doesn't instantly translate into a female version, a drag-queen-type "title" can be worked out especially for you. Aren't you excited?! Derived from some obvious or hidden aspect of your personality or person, it will be conferred upon you when you least expect it, usually when straight company is also present. As someone who is half-Asian (specifically Korean), I've been called endearingly clever names like *Jade* or *Miss Saigon* (so much for geographic accuracy).

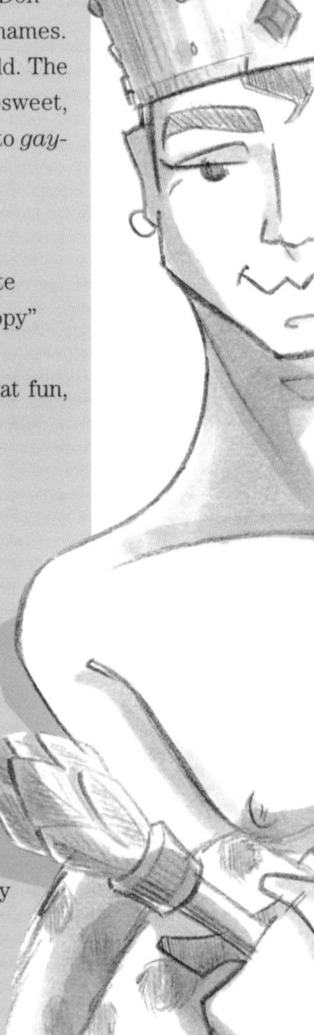

Queen for a Day

An all-time favorite bit of gay wordplay, and so damned easy even straight people can do it! First a word is chosen that best describes a person's habits, traits, or pastimes, then is joined with the word "queen." Now isn't that simple?! The combination seems to act as a "queerifier" and also gives the impression that this interest may be your one sole activity. Common examples:

drama queen (exaggerates *everything*)
opera queen (*aria* alert!)
theatre queen (responsible for turning Broadway into "The Gay White Way")
phone queen (always, *always* on one)
size queen (likes well-endowed men)
rice queen (likes Asian men; there are other names for men who prefer the company of specific ethnicities, but they tend to be rather incendiary. This one was included only because of personal experience)
label queen (wears designers only, and is also referred to as a "label whore")
dish queen (flea market lover)
cha-cha (disco) queen (loves to dance)
tone queen (as in, always setting the "right" one for dinner parties, etc.)
attitude queen (can send shivers down the spine and make your hair stand on end)

Reader Discretion Advised

Gay conversations tend to be shot all over with loads of "adult-only" innuendo—*ahem!*—but typically nothing we haven't all heard before. Someone might say, "That's too big for me," followed by the obvious, "It's not what I've heard!" But there are other ways gay men can hide blue-smelling content in front of your very nose. So think twice before you assume you've heard correctly. Below is a wad of substitute words for *aggressive (male)* to *passive (female)* sexual preferences, which can easily go unnoticed by the uninformed censor:

top *or* ***bottom***
master *or* ***slave***
pitcher *or* ***catcher***
daddy *(older) or* ***boy*** *(younger)*
chicken hawk *(older) or* ***chicken*** *(younger)*
bender *or* ***bent*** *(veddy English)*
twinkie *(a very young gay man)*
versatile *(he who plays on both sides)*

Two words—***butch*** and ***femme***—are also used by gay men to indicate how "boyish" or "girlish" anything can be from an attitude to someone's outfit. Examples: "he's trying to be too *butch*"; or "those pants make you look *femme*." Keep your ears open.

CELA VA SANS DIRE*

A gay man will go to great lengths—even "cross an ocean"—to give himself more *savoir faire*. Using French *bon mots*—because France is the home of Chanel, designer *parfums*, splendid vintages, and that *de*-vine tower—seems to be the *haute* choice, and you may notice a *soupçon* of Gallic scattered in the text of *Gaydar*. Here is a *pastiche* of French-infused sentences:

- "It really is a shame about his hair, *n'est-ce pas?"*
- "That just happens to be his boyfriend *du jour*."
- "And that, *mon Dieu,* is why he will never be a great star."
- "He woke up in bed the next morning *sans pantalons!"*
- "I know you think he looks good in it, but the style is so *outré*.
- "They really are rather too *déclassé* company, even for you."
- *"Merde!* this is the last time I buy something without trying it on first!"
- "Isn't it obvious, from the *bourgeois* taste they have in home furnishings?"
- "I suppose his *insouciant* charm comes from never having to work a day in his life."
- "Honey, you're not as *petite* around the waist as you think you are."
- "Well, a little *de trop,* but just around the edges."
- "The musical numbers were done with such *panache* I could barely stay seated!"

And the four most frequently used French words in the "gayish" language:

très (very) • ***quel(le)*** (what, who, and which)
voilà! (here or there!) • ***c'est*** (that's)

(Note: *über*-gays will also use a smattering of other languages—including German (*Danke!*), Italian (*Ciao, bambino!*), Yiddish (*Oy!*), Spanish (*Hola!*), even Latin (*Quid pro quo*)—to further distinguish themselves from the *hoi polloi*.)

* From the French, meaning, "it goes without saying."

A WORD (OR TWO) BEFORE MOVING ON

Still doubt that gay men speak a "different" language? Well, for a potent dose of dishy dialogue reality, stand anywhere near one on the telephone or, better yet, his cell phone (one of at least two) as he chatters away—like a 1950s teenager on "her" pink Princess phone in the bedroom—about the *cutest* television weathermen, sexy clothing purchases, arduous gym schedules (along with updates on muscle gains and weight losses), and loads more *pressing* inanities.

Pumpkin, nothing can get you closer to—or make you want to stand further from—his self-important orbit. Houston! We *definitely* have a problem.

On to gay behavior. How does a gay man act? Flighty, haughty, persnickety? Often forced to subvert our true nature for fear that *appearing* gay may have grossly negative repercussions—loss of jobs, friends, family—we have become masters at wearing "acceptable" disguises. Yet, no matter how adept some gay men are at covering up, they internalize very strong involuntary forces ready to jump out and strip them of their facades. Documenting many of these as "gay" idiosyncrasies—from the "skipping" walk to the "limp" wrist—infuriates those not wishing to label behavior. However, few actions can belie one's true sexual orientation with greater acuity. Yet, as a gentle reminder, to be gay does not mean one has to *act* gay. Although there is absolutely nothing wrong with that if you do!

For the next few pages, let's study a gay man in repose and action and see if we can get him—figuratively speaking—with his pants down. Over the years, some "gay" physical gestures have gone mainstream; they have not altogether disappeared, but are now imperceptible to the untrained "gay" eye. However, a willing student can be taught to catch the sleight-of-hand performed by these hunky Houdinis. We begin with . . .

GAY MAN ACTING

Gay men come in an infinite variety of personalities, but for our purposes I have chosen to illustrate only four. No doubt, this *queer*-tet of gaydom's most redoubtable, revered, recognizable, and reviled could already be among your best friends—and what a card party that would be! (Note: Good and bad, *all* gay men have a little—or a lot—of the personality traits of these four "men.")

The "Sensation"

Sexy and stylish (with a great body, no doubt!). Insightful, witty, *and* wise. Mannish and well-mannered (but not *too*). Openly, unapologetically, but not *undeniably* gay. However, being the Ken doll that he is, he may be too perfect to be around if you're having a low-self-esteem day.

The "Sweetheart"

Always there to lend a helping hand (even on moving day!), a shoulder to cry on (even when his own heart is breaking), an ear in confidence (even when you are having those illicit thoughts!), and a smile to brighten your day (with a joke that offends no one).

The "Sissy"

The assumed gay archetype. Homophobes and many gay men (called sissyphobes) hate the very thought of him. But it's their own self-recriminations and doubts which do not allow them to indulge in the pleasure of his esteemed, albeit often eccentric, company.

The "Snoot"

His aim in life is to be a constant pitiless and pernicious priss—all he can muster under his *sissy*-phean working conditions (such a rough life!)—while making you, his *friend*, feel insecure about everyone you date, everything you wear, think, and do. Treats all people like a waiter, because no one wants to wait on him.

LIGHTS, **CAMERA, ACTION!**

Gay men have no fear of anyone lurking in the bushes (or behind the couch), ready to pop out and play *paparazzi,* because we are always "camera-ready." The instantaneous pose-ability of our heads and bodies —done in such a way that only the most photogenic angles can be captured on film for posterity—can be done without missing a beat of the conversation or having anyone notice what we're up to. Now that takes real talent!

GAY MAN SITTING

Lounging can be most comfortable, but it poses problems for gay men. It is almost impossible to maintain leanness through the waist area without holding your breath, and it's difficult to show off the *derrière* at the same time you try to have eyes focused on your crotch. Yet, where there's a will there's a way. The three gay sitting positions:

The "Gidget"

Both legs bent sideways (typically shoeless or barefoot), one arm propped for balance and the other seductively stretched over the legs or crotch. This coy fellow would look right at home with a glass of wine on a bearskin rug. Very Sandra Dee. However, he *is* one quick position away from lying down, so go easy on the merlot. Caution: If the top leg is propped up and open in the "*Playgirl*" configuration, he is *undoubtedly* ready to play.

The "Clasp"

Gay men's legs are always in danger of spreading open at the most inappropriate times. That makes this second seating the most sexually secure. The look is casual but the intention is serious. One possibly errant limb is safely hooked under the other for easy but ultimate security. A popular choice at sex addicts meetings.

The "Cross-over"

A *gaydar* classic. This thigh-over-thigh crossed-leg position is elegant and refined, but still manages to tease the viewer by gently forcing the genitalia up front and center. Additionally, the more the body leans askance and legs shift diagonally, the gayer this one gets. The pinnacle position is reached when, at the end of the crossed leg, the foot is extended *en point* or a shoe is balanced off the foot in the precarious "toe-dangler." Here, reviewing the shoe itself will yield more gay clues: A current hot style? Do the socks match the shirt, pants, or footwear? All are gay, but each creates a stunningly different visual effect.

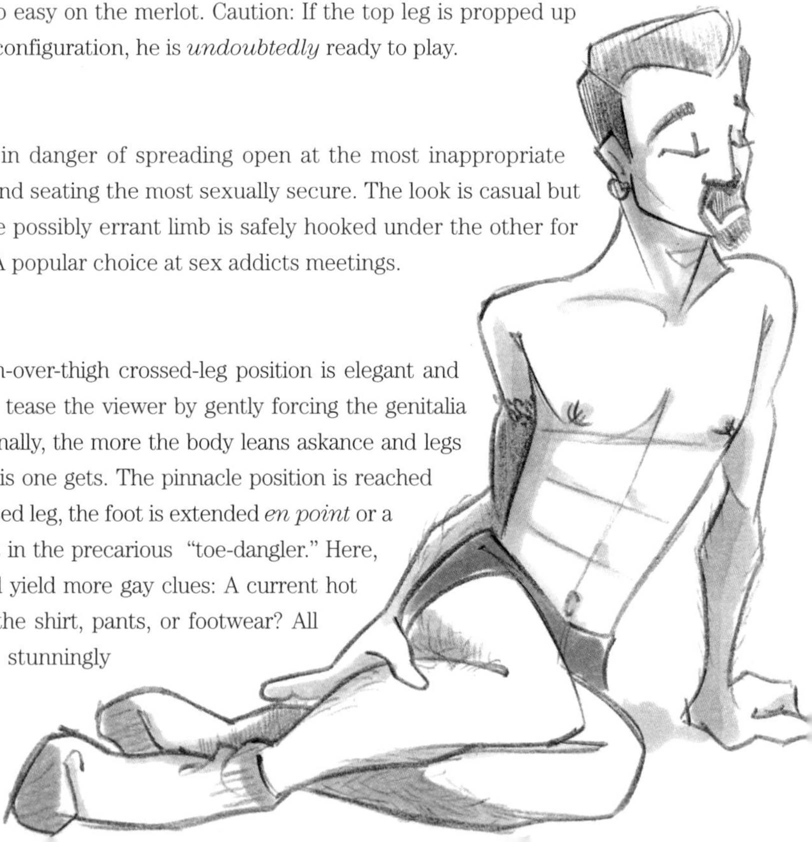

Three *gay* men in one room? How to tell? All are speaking simultaneously.

GAY MAN STANDING

Standing allows a gay man to do three things: proclaim dominion over his territory; show his availability (long or short term); and, likely the most productive use of a standing position, allow you to see his ensemble (which we pronounce *on-som-blay*) in the way that it was meant to be seen: hanging off his broad shoulders, and falling in unbroken lines to the top of his too-new-to-be-comfortable shoes. Four *out*-standing gay posits:

The "Model"

Also known as the "Christian Dior New-Look" pose (what year, fellows? see page 132) and comprising these fine points:

- the entire body is ever-so-slightly leaning, with head turned (of course) to catch the most flattering light
- shoulders back and at their broadest (unless a "sulking-pensive" mood is required)
- chest out, subtly forcing impression of a nipple to appear through clingey material of sexily unbuttoned shirt or stretch tee, or its *erectness* when shirtless
- one hand is resting on an elegantly twisted hip—a wonderful way to emphasize a slim waistline—or upraised to bring attention to the face and gently tousled hairstyle
- the other arm descending downward to compound "lean" effect
- one leg is straightened to act as center of gravity, while . . .
- the other is placed forward and gracefully *akimbo* (so-o-o divine and so-o-o Dovima! Who? See page 132)
- the body ends in appropriately shod feet, angled away from one another for balance—and to give the viewer a variety of different angles to admire the person, the pose, and the outfit

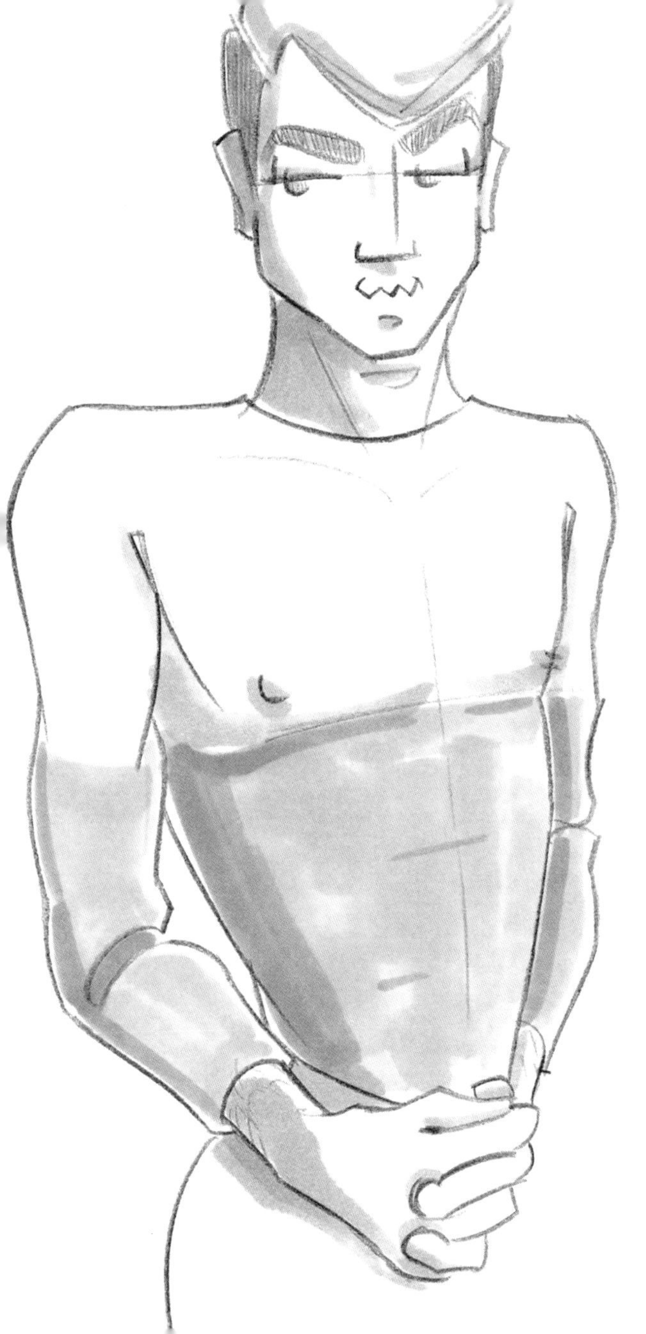

The "Uptight"

Despite the often jaunty playfulness of this dapper dandy's duds and natty accoutrements, the gentleman himself could be described as somewhat "rigid" in appearance (and I'm being delicate). Oh, what the hell, the guy looks like a rod is holding him up—and *that* ain't comfortable (let me tell you!). Other prickly indications of this Popsicle stick:

- intertwined ("laced") fingers, always placed protectively over genital area (unless arms are defiantly crossed just below the chest—even he will not cover his nipple area—in the "armor-all" position)
- shoulders back, chest out (but not nearly as teasingly as the "model"), with breath held tight (indicated by pinched facial expression) to keep stomach muscles firm and flattened
- clenched buttocks—also known as the "diamond mine" state—to deflect unwanted advances while still emphasizing roundness
- feet placed at right angles in the "Mary Poppins" stance (see illustration above)—sometimes referred to as the "Balanchine"—to secure body in one spot, until uprooting becomes absolutely necessary

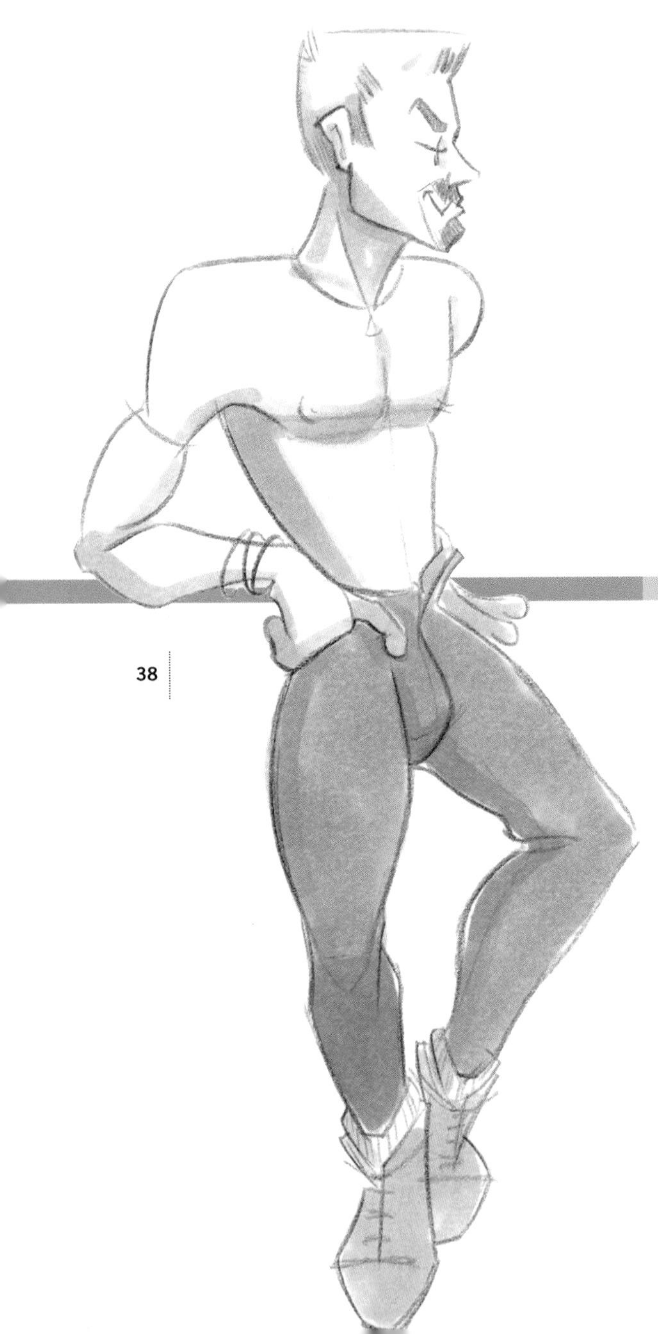

These two boys are never far from each other, and it shouldn't take much of an explanation to understand why.

The "Frontload"

Any cowpoke standing in a tight tee and torn jeans with his legs spread so wide open—sometimes with one leg up on the footrest to further encite your panting gaze—is definitely looking for something to brand with his hot poker. This attention-getting, pulse-quickening poseur would be considered the most blatantly sexual if it weren't for the obviousness of his bookend "The Backside." More protruding pronouncements:

- often hairy and muscular
- large, banana-sized produce crowding his fruit basket
- discernible "wearmarks" in front denim crotch area
- unbuttoned top button of button-front or zipper-fly jeans
- footwear limited to combat or construction boots (which do not need to be removed)
- often no belt or underwear
- unusually adept at knot-making
- a favorite song: "That's the Way I Like It" (by what gay-fave disco group? see page 132)

The "Backside"

It goes without saying that those who choose to be so up-front about their assets have left any discretion at their back door. Poured into his painted-on jeans, if you can't guess what this shameless (often shirtless) puss-in-Chelsea-boots is after *and* how he wants it when he gets it, you need to get out more (a *helluva* lot more). Further "end" results:

- often smooth and muscular
- two well-formed scoops ready for *your* banana-sized splitter (*groan*)
- discernible holes in back denim rear area
- footwear limited to slip-on (and off) shoes
- often no belt or underwear
- unusually adept at knotlike positions
- a favorite song: "Pull Up to the Bumper" (by what gay-fave dance diva? see page 132)

A Leg Up

All four aforementioned *out*-standing positions include the addition of the "floating" gay leg, used mainly for balance when picking up a set of barbells, or extending over unripened vegetables to grab at ripe ones. Sometimes swift and unexpected like a horse's kick, it is better not to stand behind this man—unless you know him intimately.

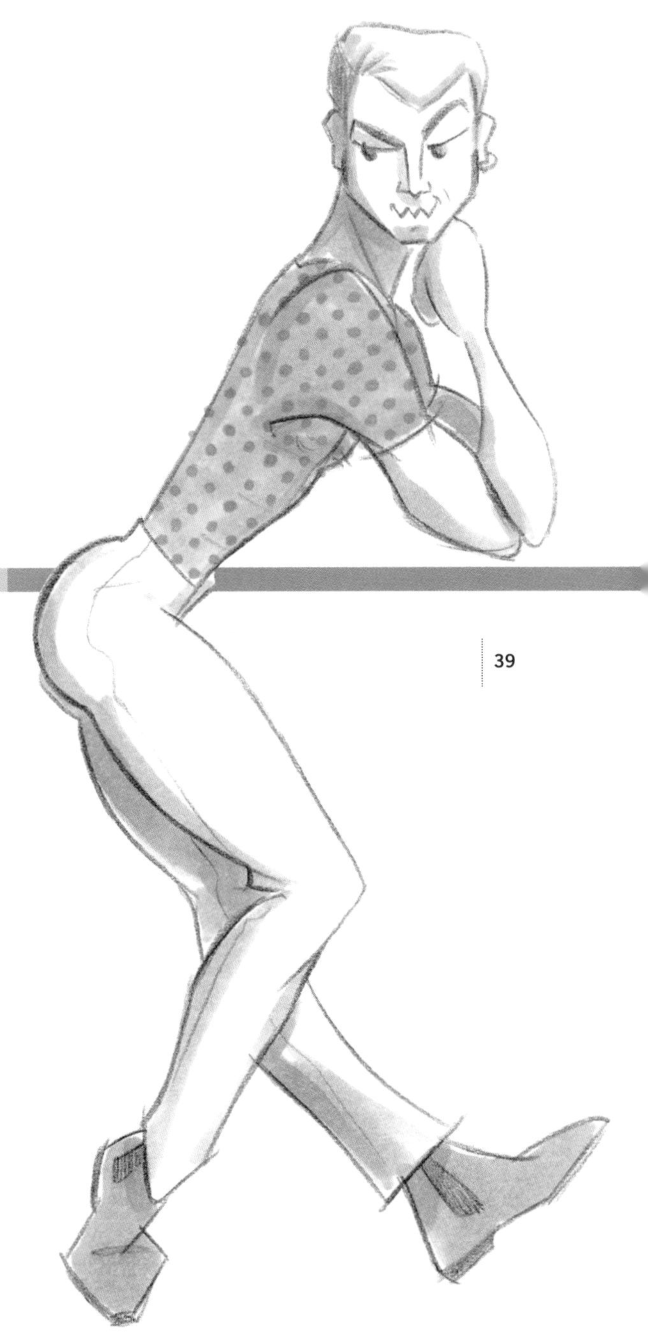

GAY MAN WALKING

If the sitting or standing gay man is too difficult to pin down—how hard can it be?—perhaps walking he will be easier to track. Certainly, a full moment or two as he strolls by gives you more to work with. But steer clear of his path when he's in a hurry; no one will mow you down faster than a gay man on a mission. The six gay gaits:

The "Broomstick"

Named for the distinct impression one gets that the walker has either a broom shoved up his you-know-what, or is *flying* on same through the room. Either way, he is an especially curt queer, full of "I-see-no-one-but-me" moxie. He is measurably more dangerous during the winter months when long, full coats are worn, and children, small animals, and curios are in peril of being swept onto the floor or under the rug. Also known as "The Wicked Witch of the West" walk.

The "Skipper"

A *gaydar* classic. This is the lope schoolchildren recognize and use as an excuse to taunt sensitive classmates with jeers like "walks like a girl" (although I have yet to see one who actually does). Grown up, his brisk canter elicits remarks about his delicate "tippy-toes" and inquiries into his obvious dancer or gymnast background. His goofier-geekier cousin: the slow-paced "Doh-De-Doh."

The "(Fashion) Runway"

This one happens only if you have the "catwalk" gene. Don't bother the attempt without it; you'll look like a straight guy with two left feet. *Scary!* This takes precise internal rhythm and the ability to walk in step, glide, and turn with—or without—actually hearing music play. By no small chance, it also happens to be a splendiforous way to show off your new glad rags. The big payoff: those marvelous turns, ending right at the bar—in "The Model" standing position—and a fresh Cosmopolitan, ready and waiting. The only drawback: needing lots of floorspace to get the whole mesmerizing effect.

The "Hitch-in-His-Get-Along"

You could get a little disoriented watching this one's tight little butt bounce up and down and from side to side, but there are lots of less-fun ways to get dizzy. You may also notice that over time Mr Muffins doesn't own a jacket or a coat with a hem ending *below* the waist. This does make him slightly easier to buy for at Christmas and birthdays. Coincidentally, "Hitch" happens to be the walk following or preceding the "The Backside."

The "Royal Highness"

The name says it all. Like watching the queen herself promenade through the room. This dandy definitely practices with books on his head when no one is watching. But, *poor dear,* with his nose up in the air like that he's an easy trip for *carelessly* placed feet and sticky floors. The tad less nasty but no less lofty cousin of "The Broomstick."

The "Breeze"

This man makes you feel like the only *breathable* air is in his company, as he gracefully and unobtrusively wends his way through a crowded, smoky room. A less self-centered version of the "Runway," he is the perfect person to go walking with.

All the above include the gay sashay bonuses of:
the curbside puddle leap
the doggy-do *(and other unspeakables)* ***sidestepper***
the imaginary "high heeler"

The striding gay man (see illustration) won't leave home without his designer messenger bag (or backpack-*slash*-gym tote)—which is always worn with the shoulder strap "cross-cleavage" style to enhance pectoral pulchritude.

GAY MAN TALKING

Gay men engaged in conversation look a lot like brightly colored birds chirping in a birdbath. A gathering of more than two will make you feel like you just arrived on the set of an Alfred Hitchcock movie. Look out, Tippi! (See page 132.) Topics? Generally speaking, flotsam and jetsam-type stuff that most likely began with the opening statement "Can you believe he . . . ?!" More animated discussions can have both men tossing their heads back, sharp peals of forced laughter, and the constant flashing of almost alien-white teeth; if you unnerve easily, you may want to exit right about now. Other signs that the "regal eagles" have landed:

rolling eyes **-** The patented "You've got to be kidding" look. Very droll and unconcerned, often very funny and *très* gay, especially in tandem with . . .

arched eyebrow(s) **-** Appears as a sign of recognition, but is usually thorny or haughty in origin. Seems to say, "Oh, *really?*" If a gay man can raise both independent of one another, he is not to be messed with by the casual or unprepared. A *gaydar* classic of the first order.

limp wrist **-** Possibly the most well known *gaydar* classic of them all, and when applicable accompanied by the weak and wimpy handshake. Followed by . . .

flailing **-** All this flapping of the hands (another *gaydar* classic) is used to visually dramatize dialogue (like a gay puppet show without the puppets). Splayed fingers (always ready to tap a chest) add credibility, and wildly gesticulating arms—a bit spastic Jackie Chan and quite lethal if you stand too close—underscore the *urgency* of the storytelling.

The "Battle" *Royale*

Gay men love to be the center of attention. Unfortunately, it isn't something you can share. This often results in a "battle" of words between men who want the spotlight. The more worthy the opponents, the more entertaining things will get (and not to missed by anyone who appreciates priceless one-liners, snappy retorts, and something that resembles a Watusi dance without the spears). Things overheard: movie awards mistakes, travel plans, clothing sale dates, exercise routines, and latest diets. (Note: Don't assume that gay men talking—even in a "battle" royale—is the same as gossiping/critiquing. *That's* another subject [see page 110].)

GAY MAN **LOOKING**

Unless a man has food on his face, is bleeding from a gunshot, or is Elvis, you will not (and *should* not) see straight men staring at one another. But gay men have taken what is a relatively harmless act—looking about *mano a mano*—and made it into a sleuthy and seductive set of at-a-glance techniques for fun, friendship, and foreplay. These looks come in various degrees of intensity, from the barely noticeable to the all-out frontal assault. Get ready, *soldiers,* the attack will likely happen with one of these four main *gay*zes:

the covert - the ever-popular sideways eye cut, often accompanied by crossed arms forcing show of viewer's formidable chest.

the lingering - shows definite interest, but a bit on the psychopathic side if it goes on too long. Hey, stud, take a picture!

the over-the-shoulder - an infamous *gaydar* classic. The six steps are: notice cute man, walk two paces past, stop, glance in store window, turn head slightly over one shoulder, look in his direction. Repeat if needed in front of next shop.

the up-and-down *or* ***once-over*** - predatory and obvious, like a large jungle cat sizing up a meal. Don't be shocked if you see the tiniest tip of a tongue and lip-licking for emphasis.

Note: The addition of an arched eyebrow to any of the above expresses added viewer interest. However, not all these stares are sexual in orientation: he may recognize you, but can't place your face; be caught up in the reverie of a recent encounter (and blocking traffic); or be just plain ditzy.

The "Gay" Evil Eye

The most dangerous gay look of them all. This invisible knife-wielding glower is intended to render the victim speechless, powerless, *and* lifeless. A Medusa-worthy *gay*ze that typically shows on the face of the renderer when he has just:

- noticed you wearing the same shirt he bought, but has not yet had a chance to wear himself
- been informed you were chosen "most stylish," when every one of his friends expected him to win
- recently discovered—by witnessing the use of one of the gay stares—that his boyfriend obviously finds you attractive

Please bear in mind that the "evil eye" is very similar in appearance to "The Gay Squint," but the two faces are very different. The squint usually occurs when the bearer has either forgotten his contact lenses; not picked up his new matte black eyeglasses and refuses to wear his old shiny black ones; or left his rose-colored Gucci sunglasses in the hotel room—in his mad dash to get a good lounging chair—and is scanning the pool area for a cocktail waiter, for any possible "next" sexual conquest, or to see if any famous person is also lying out poolside.

A "gay" occupation? Yes (but don't expect to read any confirmation in company literature). Moreover, it's not all fun-and-*gay*mes even in the gay-*friendliest* areas of income—the creative and performing arts. Even in the best of times, these rather unstable endeavors can turn some of us catty, cutthroat, and contemptuous. Not the nicest bunch around the watercooler. Nevertheless, given a choice, most of us would risk the wrath of a raving queen over optioning space within the cramped cubicles of corporate America. It also helps matters that gay occupations offer such easy access—and great discounts—to a five-way of our favorite things:

clothes • ***home decor*** • ***travel*** • ***entertainment*** • ***sex***

You may already be asking, "Does being designated a gay job mean that straight men are excluded from participating?" Hardly. Nor is it meant to negate whatever contributions they may make to a fairly "fairy" field. But more important, naming it a "gay" job in no way means that it is less worthy or difficult than earning a straight paycheck.

Three Gay Fantasy Jobs

There isn't a gay man alive who hasn't at one time or another in his life dreamt of being one of these men (hell, a lot of straight guys, too). If not personally, then he assuredly wants to marry or date one of this trio of trophy boys. Who wouldn't?!

The Pop Star **-** for the clothes, hairstyles, and new dance moves
The Movie Star **-** because you only have to work once a year (and for the sunglasses)
The Porn Star **-** Duh! because you get *paid* to have sex with impressively endowed men (hey, even a lot of *straight* men—so they claim—go "gay-for-pay").

Three "Regular Guy" Jobs We Wish Were Gay

Fireman (for the sleeping arrangements and that pole!)
Forest Ranger (for "bear" lovers!)
Gym Teacher (lesbians can't have all the fun!)

The "Siegfried and Roy" of gay laborers.

The Flight Attendant

When airlines began propagating the pretty stewardess image in the sixties—"Coffee, tea, or me?"—this job forever became thought of as a "woman's" profession. And even though men were actually the first to "work" the cabin, they were not allowed to be *re*-hired until the seventies. Today, it still takes a *special* man to travel this route. Fortunately, Mr Mile-High-in-the-Sky has the ability to keep us happy at a *cruising* altitude of 35,000 and can serve you a lot more than a hot plate of food or cold drink. Every time you climb on board, this flyboy earns his little silver wings. Ah, such *friendly* skies!

Kissing cousin: the male nurse.

The Florist

Here he is, that sturdy blossom in the flower garden of gay men. His superb handling of nature's bounty—albeit altered for balance, theme, and budget—has helped to make the *beau monde* an even rosier, and less thorny, place for everyone. True, he owes a debt to the straight men who grow the flora—and who don't mind sticking their hands into wormy dirt (yuck!)—but knows they are all thumbs when it comes to arrangements. And, *daisy darling*, without that skill you might as well just pull 'em out of the ground yourself and stick 'em in a jelly jar! Such rabble ideas!

The Fashion Designer

Gay world royalty, and this "queen's" crown goes back for generations. When King Neanderthal needed clothes (and an opinion), a gay cave prince was likely standing by with pelt, needle, and thread in hand. However, most gay men are not related to fashion's royal family. Born without the necessary genes, we assume *buying* the latest pair will get us into the palace. I don't think so, girlfriend!

In the dressing room: the costume designer and the wardrobe supervisor.

The Apparel Buyer

Without this man none of the Prince of Fashion's wares would end up in our closets. But don't dismiss him as a glorified shopper—still, paid to shop?!—it's really only fun if you get to buy sexy menswear.

Gaydar 101: Fashion Forecasting

Some are born fashion prophets, but *anyone* can predict the next hot trend. How? Simple. It's almost always a look opposite from the one before: short-long; tight-loose; '70s-'80s. Hot designer? If he works for a once-great couture house ready for relaunch—*and* if he's a hottie—the hotter the chances of success.

The Interior Designer

Would we know the difference between chintz and chintzy, where to toss a throw pillow, or the available tiles for that backsplash if it weren't for this informed fellow and his swatch books? I think not. And who else could utter lines like "That shade of puce is perfect for the vestibule!" to indecisive homeowners—while keeping a *straight* face? (Who else but a gay interior designer would think to speak such innocuous but seemingly life-altering statements?) Certainly, under the circumstances, everyone can agree with this simply put statement, "Mary, it takes a fairy to make something pretty!" (Can you name the gay decorator who said this and the film. See page 132 for the answers.)

In the wings: the window, set, and production designer.

The Antique Dealer

The mustier, dustier, paler (from lack of sunlight), and frequently curmudgeonly cousin of the above. This gay gatekeeper of the glorious past separates the quaint from the antiquated, the curio from the curiosity, and has "hands-on" access to the valuable "hands-off" item you simply must have for your foyer demilune.

This comely quartet keeps the creative and performing communities alive, well, and safe. Without their cultivation, all artistic flames—and little flamers—would extinguish themselves, leaving us in the cultural darkness of reality TV, tabloid news, and funniest home videos.

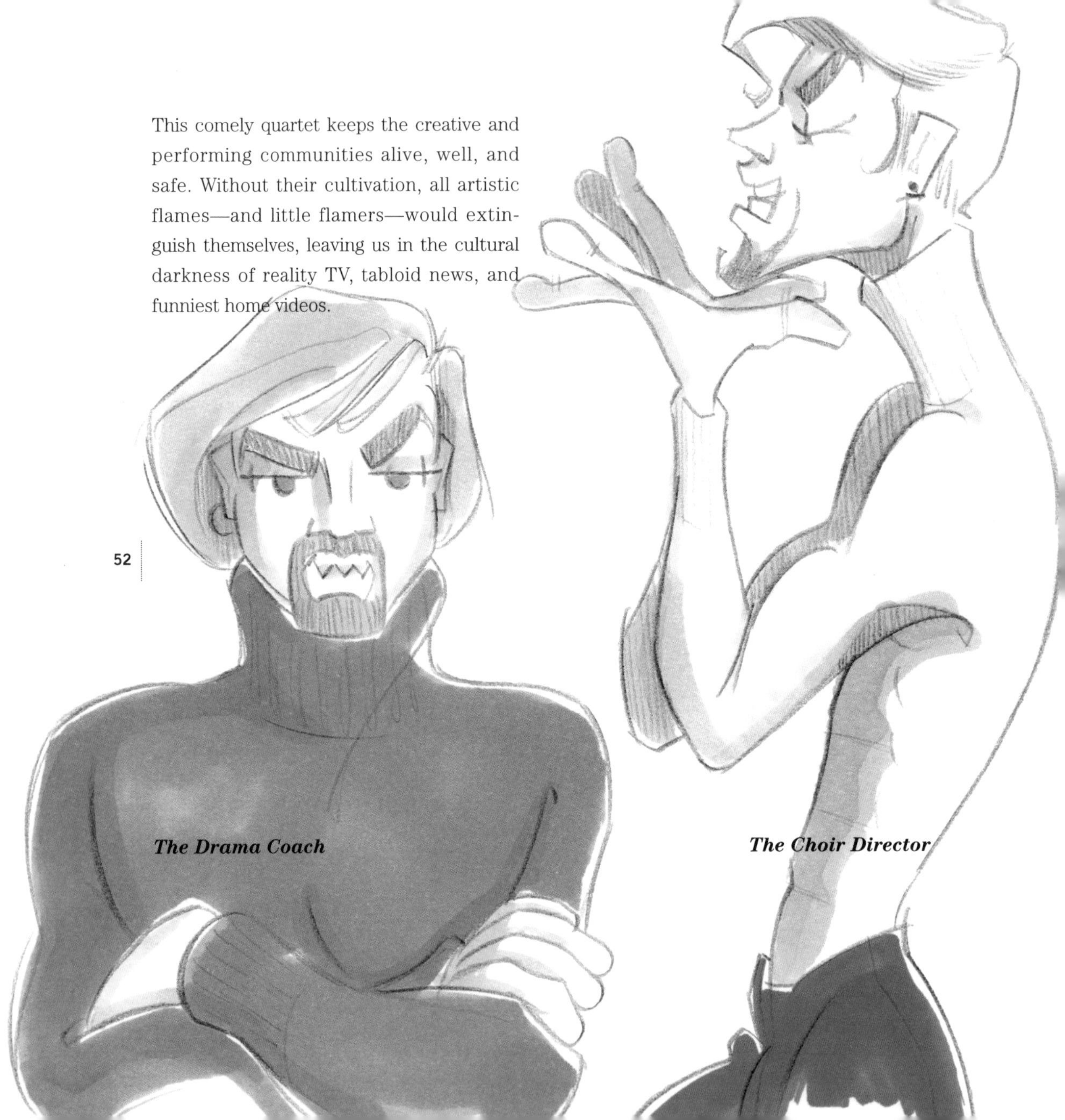

The Drama Coach

The Choir Director

The Theatre Manager

The Museum Curator

The Publicist
The Party Planner
The Personal Assistant
The Concierge

In the gay world—where knowing who's who, what's what, and where to go to find both is paramount—this band of "Mary" men are at the top of the heap. Remarkably, even the most "in-the-know" A-list gays (and straights, alike) would *not* know whom to invite to their shows, parties, and openings; arrive late at said functions given by others *and* themselves; eat in the wrong eateries (or order the wrong meal in the right ones); and buy tickets to closed shows if not for the able aid of one of these four. Unfortunately, keeping track of such numbingly fast-changing information makes this quartet the most harried and neurotic of all gay speciality workers. Nevertheless, get on the good side of any and you will find yourself shuffling through engraved (or ingeniously designed) invitations to the best open-bar parties, gallery shows, movie openings, and awards banquets in town. Get on any bad side, and you may never play in this town again. Note: This group is assembled in no particular order of importance, whatsoever!

Queer

The Clothing Stylist
The Hair Stylist
The Makeup Artist
The Art Director

What percentage of the way "Miss-or-Mr-of-the-Moment" looks *at this moment* do you think has anything to do with her/his own personal style—the way she/he sits, acts, speaks—or taste in clothes, makeup, hair? We may never get an accurate answer to this question. Ask one of these four, you will get a *Rashomon**-like response: each will have his own take on the story—and may take more credit than due. Regardless, few stars and models (female *and* male) could look as good as they do without them running interference (or interfering!). The secrets they've kept and the things they have seen could fill the pages of a book—I think the title *Beauty and the Beastly* is quite apropos.

Note: Until straight men can be trusted in the dressing rooms of naked women—with or without big bosoms—these four men will remain overwhelmingly gay. (And yes, in answer to the obvious follow-up question, we can be trusted—*barely*—in a room full of naked men.)

* Know the film? See page 132.

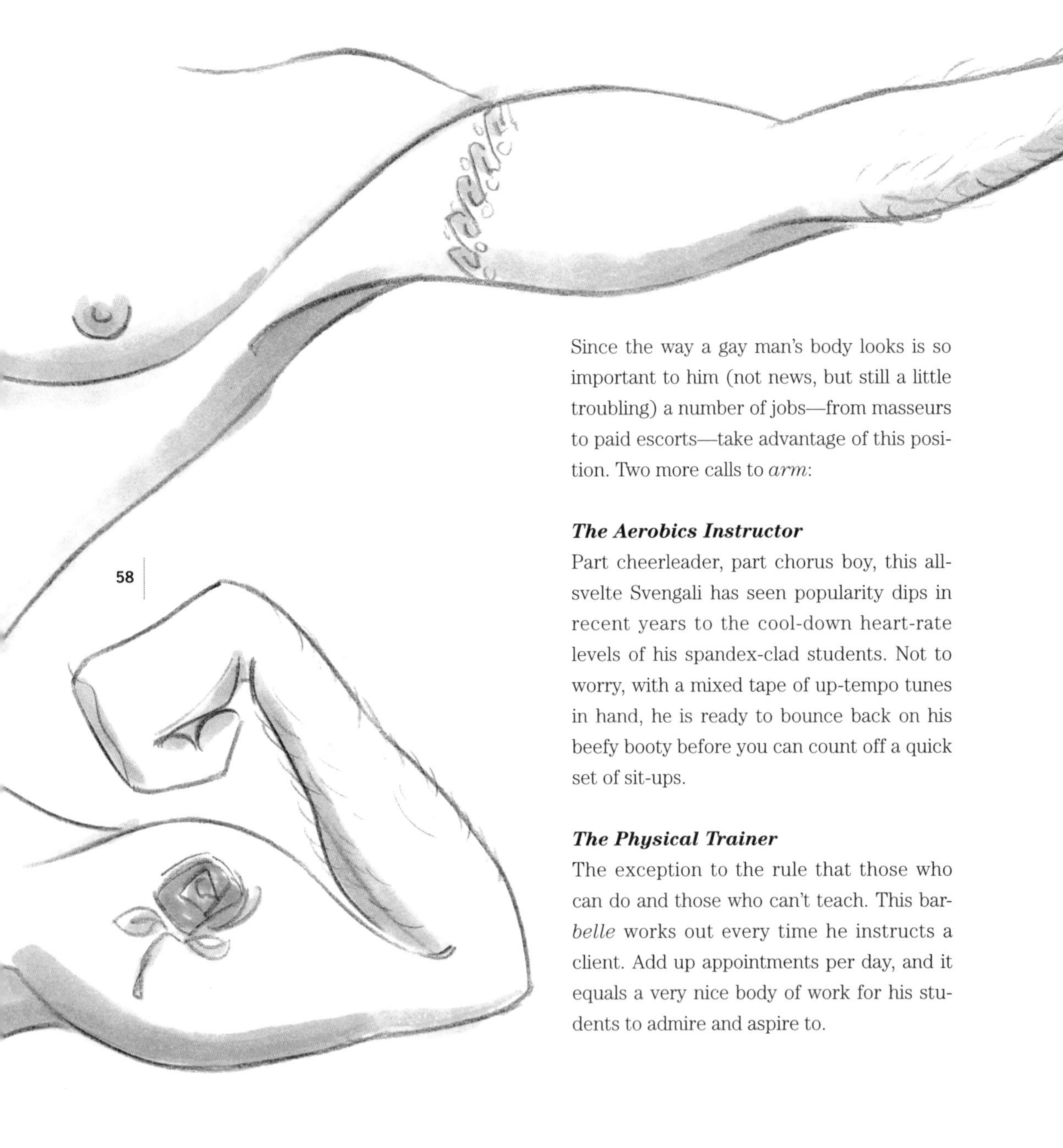

Since the way a gay man's body looks is so important to him (not news, but still a little troubling) a number of jobs—from masseurs to paid escorts—take advantage of this position. Two more calls to *arm*:

The Aerobics Instructor

Part cheerleader, part chorus boy, this all-svelte Svengali has seen popularity dips in recent years to the cool-down heart-rate levels of his spandex-clad students. Not to worry, with a mixed tape of up-tempo tunes in hand, he is ready to bounce back on his beefy booty before you can count off a quick set of sit-ups.

The Physical Trainer

The exception to the rule that those who can do and those who can't teach. This bar-*belle* works out every time he instructs a client. Add up appointments per day, and it equals a very nice body of work for his students to admire and aspire to.

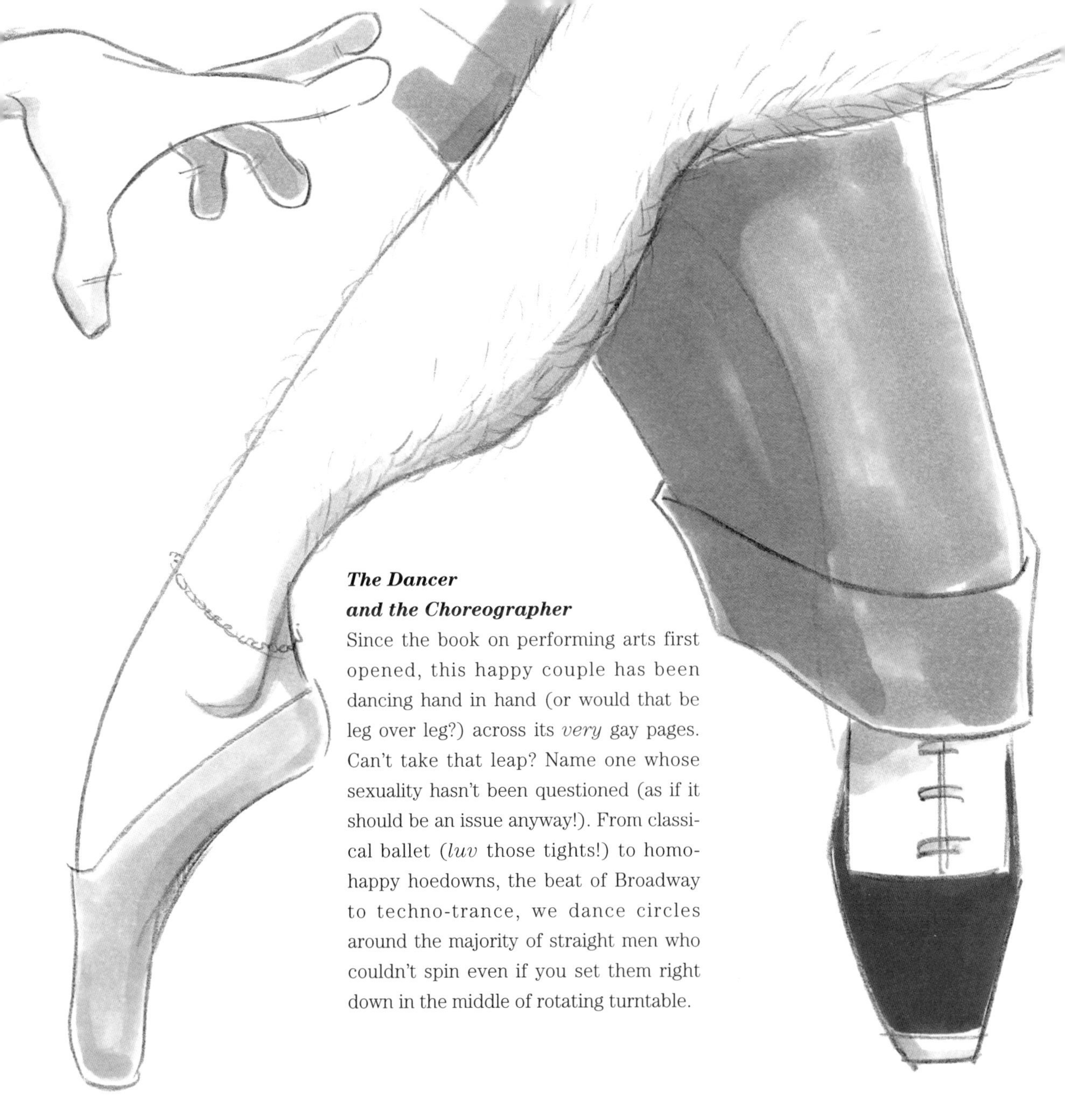

The Dancer and the Choreographer

Since the book on performing arts first opened, this happy couple has been dancing hand in hand (or would that be leg over leg?) across its *very* gay pages. Can't take that leap? Name one whose sexuality hasn't been questioned (as if it should be an issue anyway!). From classical ballet (*luv* those tights!) to homo-happy hoedowns, the beat of Broadway to techno-trance, we dance circles around the majority of straight men who couldn't spin even if you set them right down in the middle of rotating turntable.

Gay men actually appear to like waiting on people. In particular, we show up in great numbers and do quite well as one of these service-oriented *professionals*:

The Salesclerk - stylish *and* attentive
The Waiter - quick-witted *and* nimble
The Bartender - fast on his feet *and* shirtless
The Go-Go Boy - amenable *and* accessible

For nearly every young gay man, one of these will serve as a right-of-passage into greater gaydom's world of partying, party clothes, and paying rent. It should also lead to a *real* profession—one he can actually tell his mother about—and fame and fortune (at least enough so that he can afford a summer share with his friends). Even after leaving servitude far behind, you can still espy traces of his table-waiting days as he swiftly maneuvers around guests with stacked-high trays of cracked crab, gathered by his pool in Palm Springs. Note: Until straight men are comfortable serving gay men—likely never to occur in any significant numbers—it is left for *us* to serve *them* their food, liquor, clothes, and yes, even sex (though no "straight" man would ever admit *that* ever happens!).

The Gay Career Guy in a Straight Working World

Not every gay man can work a gay job—*sister,* he may not want one or have the choice!—and might actually be happy spinning alongside millions of straight worker bees who drone on day after day in the hives of commerce and industry. Even so, intentionally or not, he can't help but stand out in his surroundings. Ways to spot the gay blade in a sea of straight grass:

- Stall decorations: Christmas tinsel, Valentine hearts, discreetly placed stuffed toys.
- Adored by all female assistants; avoided by all overtly machismo male coworkers.
- Wears the best outfits in the office (ties and socks will color-coordinate).
- Occasionally speaks in softened tones on the telephone; uses names like "bunny" or "pumpkin" in these conversations.
- Has keen, valued opinion on stars' appearances from previous night's television programming; (when asked) has keen, valued opinion of fellow workers' appearances every day.
- A stocked candy jar (Twizzlers, Jolly Ranchers, et al.) kept by the entrance to his space, for one and all to enjoy; meant as sweet excuse for same to drop by, stop, and chitchat.
- Neatens work space before leaving for the day; would straighten yours if asked.
- Hesitant to join Super Bowl pool; may start one for the Oscars.
- Refrains from making off-color remarks at the expense of others; might choose to ignore hearing those made by others.
- First to leave office/work party; may not show up at all.

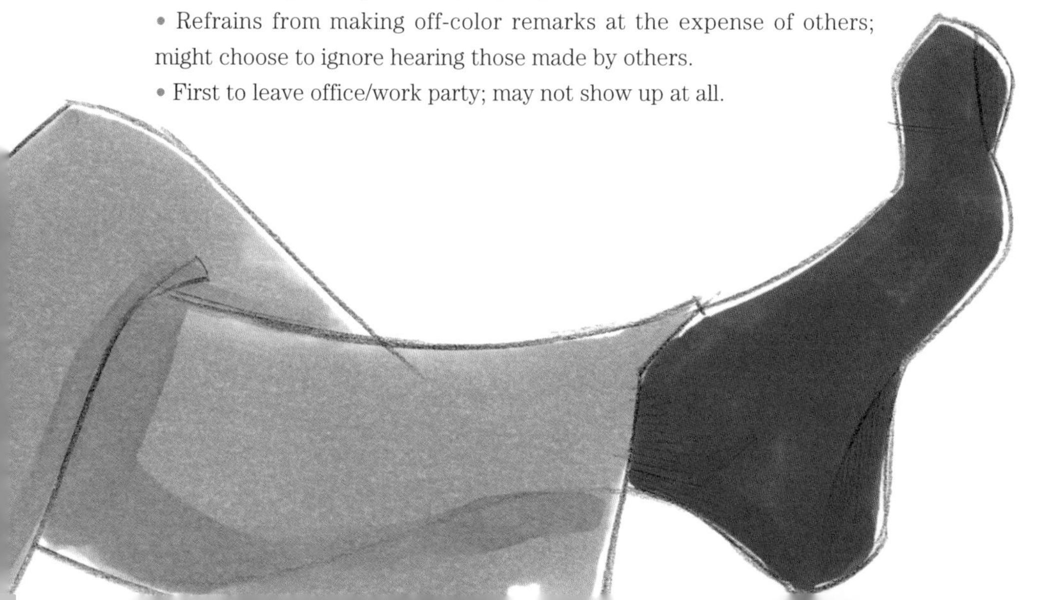

A gay man's home is his castle, and in it he reigns supreme. Moreover, many "queens" expect that through some *royal* gay birthright—following the same assumed blue-bloodlines which make us instant and impeccable clotheshorses, menu planners, and movie critics—we all automatically inherit diverting decor decorum. Doubtful. Nevertheless, if you are fortunate enough to be invited *en suite*—and obvious or not, it will be "by invitation only"—you can amply verify his vast knowledge of texture interplay, sumptuous seating, and exotic woods.

In this well-appointed place of residence you can also view a gay man's sexual predilection in all its unabashed or understated glory (especially if you stumble upon the porn stash—and *every* gay man has one). That is, unless he has found it necessary to "de-fag" the place before you arrive. This is a rather indelicately though suitably named situation in which *all* gay men have found themselves at one time or another: ridding the place of all signs of obvious homosexuality—*in flagrante delicto* refrigerator magnets, nude male picture books, and "wrestling" videos—so as not to offend visiting relatives. Not until the guests are safely back on the road will it be allowable for these items to be seen again.

Where Is He?

A great place to find a gay man may be right under your feet. Answer this: In what city is he? (Note: A gay man's home will rarely be in the same town he was born.) Pinpointing the neighborhood will give you even more undisputable evidence—and you may find that every major city in the country (and across the world) has a "gay ghetto" (an unfortunate term for an inner-city neighborhood gentrified by enterprising and economical gay men). Here are a dozen "happy" spots on the domestic map:

Chelsea (New York City)
The Castro (San Francisco)
Midtown (Atlanta)
Lakeview (Boys Town) (Chicago)
West Hollywood (Los Angeles)
Montrose (Houston)
South End (Boston)
Hillcrest (San Diego)
South Beach (Miami)
Wilton Manors (Ft. Lauderdale)
Center City (Philadelphia)
Dupont Circle (Washington, D.C.)

The 6 "P"s of Gay Home Decorating Themes

practical - decorated with economy in mind, but still delightful
proper - traditional mode decorating with updated edges
posh - indulgent and lavish, but not excessive
pretty - what the inside of all gay houses are expected to look like
precious - slightly matronly, overstuffed
pretentious - a designer-stamped showcase. Like a page out of *Elle Decor*.

The Gay Kitsch-Instinct

In addition to the above decor themes, every gay man—no matter how serious he is on the *outside*—allows at least one element of kitsch ("camp") *inside* his home (or office). If not, the man is somewhat *gay*-sthetically challenged and needs a juicy jab of *queer*-ification, fast! True, a little lava lamp levity goes a long way, but who can say no to toasting tea dance time with a tiki glass cocktail, a beefy burger done the "big boy" way, or a delirious dip in the "drag-bag"? We have this inate understanding of the irreverent reverence of kitschy humor (wasn't she a friend of Hiawatha?) for a reason—remember, they call us *gay!*—and while not every one of us could actually stand to "live" in *Green Acres,* we become "gay bores" without it.

The Gay Decor "Triple Play"

Two may be company, but a trio is definitely a crowd-pleaser when it comes to home *gay*-dorning techniques. You will spot many examples of this—from the subtle tryst of a wall hanging, vase, and table, to a flashy threesome of like-inspired *objets d'art*. We just love our three-ways!

The 8 **Gayest** Items of Home Decor

Every room in a gay man's house can yield some obvious (and some not so) pieces-a-plenty that expose his sexual orientation. Spotting any one of these eight items will get you just that much closer to ascertaining the truth. (But honestly, *sweetie-pie,* by being *inside* his house, haven't you gotten warm already?!)

potpourri

Dried flowers, berries, nuts, the occasional slice of fruit, and always scented to match the time of year. To make more gay "scents" (hyuck! hyuck!) potpourri also needs the appropriate container. Think of a large silver/crystal bowl smartly juxtaposed with books on the coffee table, or a handmade twig basket strategically placed on top of a bathroom shelving unit. Just dandy!

candles

Nowadays, they are everywhere and perilously tread the line between *gay*-sentials and "mall-merchandising-for-the-masses." No doubt, our fondness for wax will wane soon. Until then we still have a wide array to roil through, including:

- *tabletop taper*—for a romantic evening, sometimes in stripes, and *always* lit if you're going for mood.
- *cylinder*—those big, thick numbers (is it hot in here?!) set in the middle of a harvest medley or holly berry centerpiece and *rarely* lit. These are for decoration only, sugar!
- *shaped miniature*—typically animals dressed in holiday clothes with the wick sticking out of the top of their cute little heads. *Gay*-ly placed on shelves and *never* lit.

• *self-contained*—costing a day's salary and available in a variety of odors, from marvelously merry to mind-bogglingly miasmic.

objets d'art of nude men

Whether as statuary, in or on the cover of a book, painting, Polaroid, postcard, or all of the above, nude men fall into the "so-obvious-that-if-you-didn't-already-know-this-you-really-did-need-*Gaydar*-the-book-for-help" category.

coffee table books

No, *silly,* not every coffee table book is gay—those on race cars, airplanes, cities from the air, and *Playboy* bunnies make great beer mug coasters for straight men—but plop down next to a table piled high with such scintillating subject matter as fashion and film (one on Audrey Hepburn could be both and thus a space saver), flora and fauna, and the all-important glossy male nude pictorial (see above) and you have just seated yourself in *l'habitat homo.* (Gay decorating gone too far: illustrated books opened to a particular page for visual effect.)

magazines

Like coffee table books, magazines aren't actually "gay" (unless, of course, they say they are). However, don't doubt that your host *is* if you happen to glance upon more than one of these glam glossies out on display:

Vanity Fair • Metropolitan Home • Elle Decor • W
Entertainment Weekly • Men's Fitness • Gourmet
House & Garden • Martha Stewart Living • People
Travel & Leisure • Interview • Wallpaper • InStyle

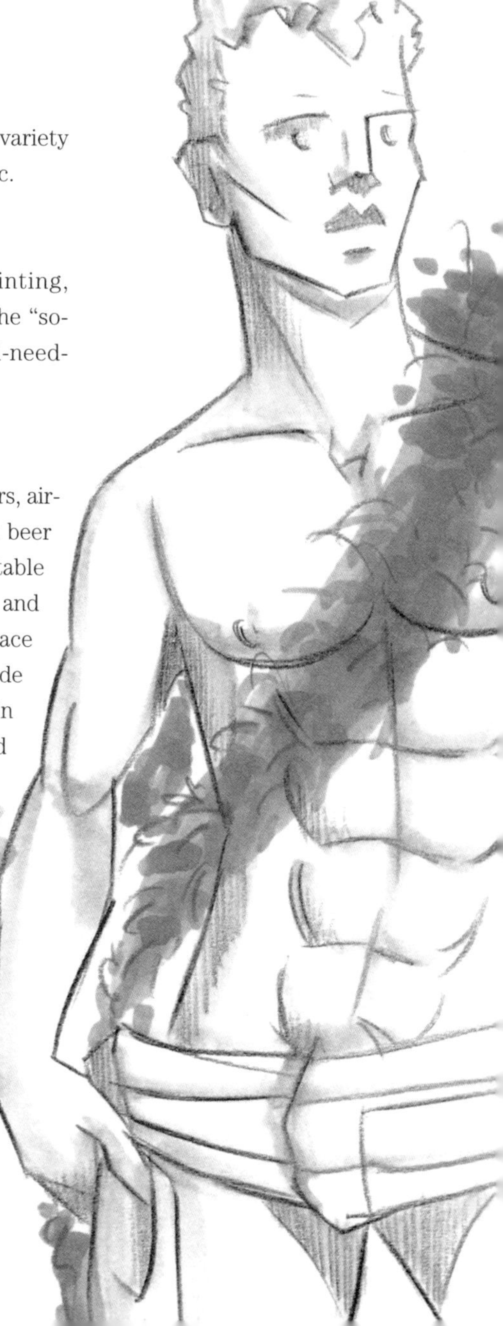

throw rugs and accent pillows

Or the reverse, accent rugs and throw pillows. The difference has everything to do with the size of one and/or the color of another. The possible combinations (and breathtaking results) are endless. If you have the time, stop by a gay man's house and take a look for yourself.

stuffed animals

A teeny-weeny tossed teddy (a little worse for the wear) from back in his childhood days doesn't mean a thing. But a whole shelf full (or bed full) of assorted ones (from bears to bunnies), old or brand-spanking new, is definitely cause for gay comment. And if any of them has a name, well, don't make *me* say it.

bric-a-brac

Also known as tchotchkes and knickknackery, and usually placed about the home's tabletops and shelves in massive, dust-gathering quantities ready to turn your ass into that of a china shop bull. (Frequently found in the same home of the man who owns shaped miniature candles.)

HOUSE PETS

Gay men often turn to the animal kingdom for companionship—*and* the ultimate household accessory. Dogs especially make excellent, nonopinionated listeners, and are great for breaking the ice on cold winter walks when Mr Perfect Pecs and his pooch happen by. If it weren't for the occasional odoriferousness of them, stray hairs on the mohair-covered sofa, and constitutionals in *bad* weather, every gay man would own one (and, hey, Coach and Gucci have some really *dee-voon* dog accessories). (Note: Small, "toy," rare-breed dogs, and too-large—*overcompensating*—dogs are very gay. Medium-sized are sexuality neutral.) Cats tend to be the gayest pets of all. However, the frequent surprise allergy attacks from one of daddy's "latest" boyfriends often makes them a too-big gamble to take. Sorry, Fluffy.

The best way to fully comprehend what a gay man's home looks like would involve a walking tour. Let's try one "virtual-style":

In his entrance foyer

- subtle, warm, and welcoming indirect, pinspot, or sconce lighting
- umbrella holder (with Burberry umbrella)
- minimal indication of overall house decor through use of single framed poster art or wall painted in coordinated color
- gilt-frame mirror (for a quick first or last look) above . . .
- console (or demilune) table, free of objects except single floral arrangement

In his living room

- deep sofa, long enough to lie down on without bending at the knee or ankle
- assorted accent pillows for show, and some to throw on floor for "casual" seating
- coordinated end table(s), topped with low-wattage light(s), books and/or magazines
- magazine rack with Neiman Marcus, Gump's, and J. Crew catalogs
- a Mitchell Gold easychair or sofa
- area rug(s) integrating basic design motifs, often atop . . .
- large-area covering neutral-color sisal rug
- state-of-the-art television, VCR, DVD, and DVR players, concealed in Oriental or '50s *Moderne* armoire, or resting atop low swivel base
- expensive poster art (in one theme)
- pencil studies (male nudes)
- glass-topped coffee table, low to accommodate casual seating. On top . . .
- crystal, hardwood, or unusual metal bowls holding stones, wooden fruit, or potpourri
- tall, phallus-shaped vase, containing not-overly-floral floral arrangement
- coffee table books (of course)
- cleverly concealed coaster container

and generally strewn about:

- leather-covered and miniature boxes
- witty curios
- scented, self-contained candles

Music plays an important part in creating the right mood in a gay home. His living room will house state-of-the-art designed and engineered music equipment—small in size to allow for optimal placement choices—which takes full advantage of his gay ambience-setting talents. Whether for a casual or formal fete—with a nod to the season—he can select the perfect background track(s) to fit any occasion:

Christmas: Vince Guaraldi's Charlie Brown
romantic: Patsy Cline
winter cocktails: Enya
summer cocktails: bossa nova*
getting ready to go out: Madonna
small party: nostalgic top forty
large party: pre-mixed top forty/dance
alone: original Broadway cast recordings

Throughout the year, elements in this room may be altered or changed to reflect "special" occasions: vintage Santas and holly-scented candles for Christmas; fall harvest cornucopias; "fresh" fruit in wooden bowls for spring; rainbow flags for Gay Pride, etc.

* What does "bossa nova" mean, and name an artist? See page 132.

In his dining room

- glass-, marble-, or brushed-metal-topped dining table with seasonal centerpiece
- table-centered lighting with dimmer switch
- seating for four (or more) in matched hardwood or tieback covered in neutral-color fabric
- decor-color-coordinated dinner plates, napkins, and napkins rings
- sideboard, china cabinet, hutch, credenza, or glass vitrine to hold extra-special dinnerware, precious objets d'art, and top-of-the-line bottles of spirits and liqueurs
- ample supply of cocktail, wine, cordial (*aperitif*), old-fashioned, beer, sherry, shot glasses and stemware

Be on extra alert for:

- charger plates
- demitasse spoons
- placecard holders/napkin rings

And if he ever uses the words "drapes" (instead of "curtains") and "swag" when describing the softly romantic mood that has been created in this (or any other) room in his house.

In his kitchen

- refrigerator magnets holding pictures of self, male friends, gallery and party invitations
- portable phone and miniature television
- small, festive floral arrangement
- cookbooks (*The Joy of Cooking,* Julia Child, Spago's, etc.) and cooking magazines
- assorted earthenware spice jars
- infinite variety of herbs and spices
- cappuccino and coffee maker
- industrial-strength blender and food processor (for fruit smoothies, power drink and margarita making)
- fancy and casual silverware
- fancy and casual dinnerware
- assorted placemats to match casual, fancy dinnerware
- mugs from Broadway plays, human rights organizations, and charities
- top-of-the-line cookware and cutlery
- soufflé dishes, assorted cake pans and muffin tins, and icing funnels (with assorted tips)
- assorted whisks, food thermometers, strainers, corkscrews, food brushes, melon ballers, peelers, presses, corn holders, zesters, chip clips
- collectible objects: salt & pepper shakers, figurines, etc.
- matching oven mitts and tea towels
- scented, self-contained candles

In his refrigerator

- spring water, diet soda, and energy drinks
- assorted juices (cranberry, grapefruit, orange, tomato, mango, and mixed)
- salad fixings and low-fat dressings
- boneless chicken breasts, fresh fish (salmon), extralean meat, green market vegetables and fruits, and homemade pasta
- top-of-the-line vodka
- limes and lemons
- olives and maraschino cherries
- party "favors" and poppers
- sorbet
- plenty of ice cubes

Food for Thought

Gay men have a sneaky relationship with food. We shout the virtues of a healthy diet, yet secretly smuggle bags of *regular* Lay's potato chips, boxes of Geno's pizza rolls, and sacks of McDonald's into our apartment and hide chocolate-chocolate-chip Häagen-Dazs in the freezer. With our toned bodies as evidence, we think you will suspect something untoward if you knew the truth that, yes, once in a while gay men actually eat like real folk. Men, no one believes you can live by rabbit food and chicken feed alone. *Girls,* gourmand guilt does not aid in digestion. So eat, already!

In his bedroom

- bed with "queen"-size mattress
- biweekly rotating sets of designer, color-coordinated bed linens
- assorted accent pillows
- assorted stuffed animals
- bedside phone and answering machine
- large armoire filled with multiple multi-color sweaters and tight T-shirts, and amply stocked sock and undies drawers, in addition to . . .
- stuffed, but organized, walk-in closet
- half-read bestselling hardcover book, *Vanity Fair,* and/or J. Crew catalogue
- concealed television; mainly for viewing Saturday-morning cartoons, late-night *Golden Girls* reruns, "gay-fave" films on cable, and VCR or DVD player (with small selection of favorite porn movies stacked, but hidden, nearby)
- additional pornography (magazines) under the bed, on a high shelf in the closet, or in the drawer of nightstand (also housing lubricants, condoms, and hand towels)
- scented, self-contained candles

Additional points:

- the sham pillow

In his bathroom

- weekly rotating sets of "super-plush" designer towels, color-coordinated with the bathmat and shower curtain
- four mirrors: one ample-sized, over sink; one small side retractable; one in-the-shower shaving; and one handheld (to check for cowlicks, areas for touch-up, and hair loss).
- fragranced and 100% fragrance-free shampoos for: highlighted, extracleansing, thinning, chemically treated, and "normal" hair.
- four types of soap: 99.9% pure, rinses without residue, antibacterial, and moisturizing (just to be clean) soap; sold at fine stores only, organic or important-sounding chemical ingredients, generically packaged (Kiehl's) or fancifully paper-wrapped (Fresh) soap; fruit, floral, or fabulous fungi-like-scented soap; and teeny-weeny, colored (for guests only or show) soap.
- assorted boar bristle hairbrushes and hard rubber combs
- clippers, tweezers, nail files, *and* an eyelash curler
- undereye circle creams
- assorted potions and lotions for general grooming from Kiehl's
- countless bottles of partially used to near-empty suntan products, including self-tanners and bronzers
- "personal" lubricants and cleansing products
- Biore deep-cleansing facial strips
- ultrawhitening toothpaste
- sonic-powered toothbrush
- spare toothbrushes (for, so he demurely says, the unexpected guest)
- wrinkle cream
- blow dryer and curling iron
- *objet d'art* atop toilet tank
- small, intimate photographs
- scented, self-contained candles

The "Mary" Medicine Cabinet

There is possibly no faster way to tell if a man is gay than a quick "strip search" of his bathroom cabinetry. There is much credibility to this statement; we have all seen the scenario played out on TV and films, and have all done a bit of under-sink breaking and entering in our day. In addition to uncovering sanitary or sloppy habits—and the discovery that he is dangerously low on lube or toilet paper—exposing certain items to the light of day can turn them into bright beacons which bare his most "secret" secrets. Unrefutable evidence: any product that by manufacturer (Clairol, Chanel, et al.) or usage (hair highlighter, eye creams, etc.) would be considered "made for women."

gay body

Gay man; perfect body? Blame it on years of pectoral propaganda—thanks to envious straight men, frustrated straight women, and our own gay body fascists—but everyone is under the impression that all gay men are walking demi-gods. In reality, walk into any gym locker room (or strip of "gay" beach) and you will be treated to a menagerie of muscled *and* muscularly challenged men. We do have a proportionately larger percentage of those who are well built. But there are solid reasons why this is so:

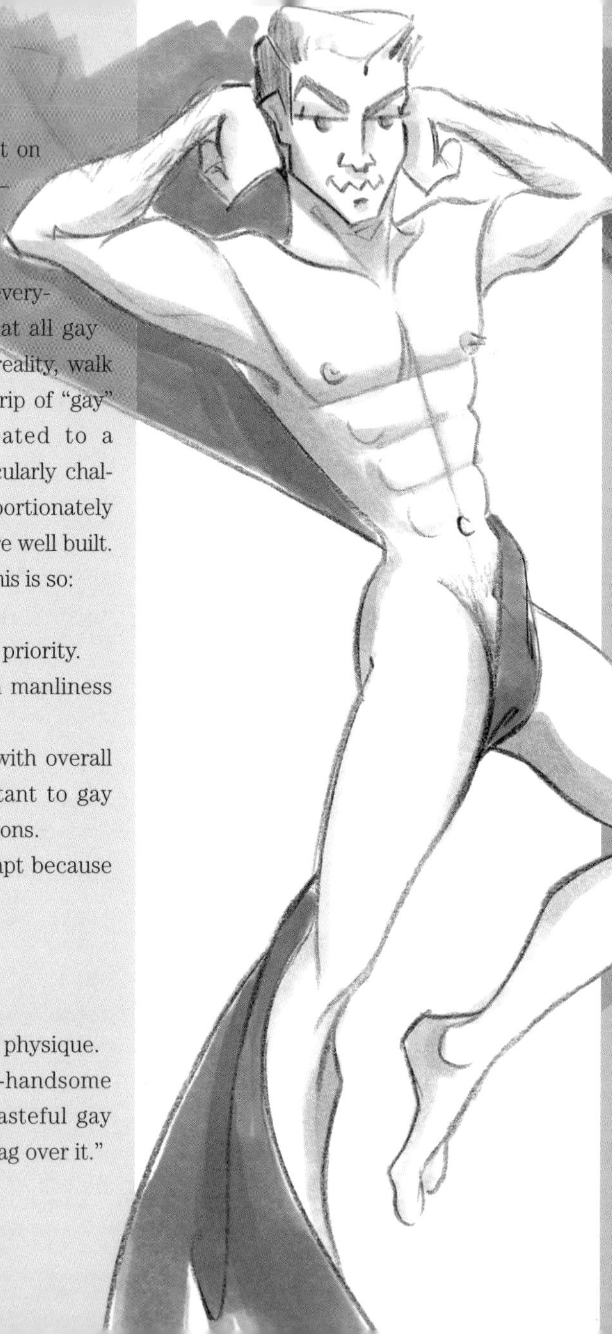

- Our lifestyles allow this to be a priority.
- A great body is equated with manliness and masculinity.
- A great body is also equated with overall good health, and this is important to gay men for (hopefully) obvious reasons.
- We frequently *make* the attempt because of the above three.

And some solidly less so:

- Clothes hang better on a toned physique.
- Compensates for a less-than-handsome face, which will beget the distasteful gay fave line, "You can always put a bag over it."
- They're *so* pretty to look at.

If there was a "perfect" gay body, it would have in luscious detail:

- ***broad shoulders and back*** - like an Olympic swimmer
- ***bulging biceps and triceps*** - but only big enough to fill out the narrowed cuff of a sexy-and-tight short-sleeve Raymond Dragon T-shirt (but never stretching it out of shape!)
- ***hairy, veiny, and large forearms*** - a "secret" gay-fave body part (but nothing too Popeye-like)
- ***big, big hands*** - because you know what that means! (If you don't, time to climb out from under that rock!)
- ***a great set of pecs*** - not as large as throw pillows, but certainly big enough for a person to cup his hands around
- ***a long, lean torso*** - with a superb set (need you be reminded) of six-pack abs. I have the image of Brad Pitt in my head.
- ***a wasp waist*** - to give us that dynamic V-shape (in a size number less than our ages)
- ***slim hips*** - almost as small as our impossibly tiny waists
- ***an unbelievably high, firm, and round booty*** - the size of two cantaloupes, not a pair of basketballs
- ***power-built legs*** - with thighs in diameter near to our waist size (no doubt, from all that dancing and in-line skating)
- ***especially well-defined calves*** - the other secret gay-fave body part—and thinnish ankles (thick ones make your legs look like tree stumps)
- ***big feet*** - because, again, you know what that means, with long toes (which some say is a sign of intelligence)

Did you notice how discreet I was by *not* mentioning size of sexual endowment? Of course if I had brought it up, you'd know that it would be substantial. (Think "Dirk Diggler" [from what film? see page 132].) But my lips are staying sealed around this one!

GYM DANDIES

Unless you have the wherewithal to *hire* an at-home trainer (ohhh, aren't we special) it usually takes outside help to become the perfect specimen of gay manhood. (Can a anyone stand the guys *born* that way?!) This is very likely going to occur in the gay world's favorite place of worship: the gym. Beyond the sweat, sinew, and steam-room sexcapades (you did know that already, right?!), these temples of testosterone are an excellent spot for exchanging decorating tips (while crunching abdominal muscles), spreading juicy tales and tidbits (on the stationary bike)—*and* you get the added bonus of watching cutie-pie strip naked in the locker room (*quel* fun!).

A "spotting" pair of gay gym patrons:

The gym rat - This beefy and bellicose behemoth is always at the gym (does he live there?!), grunting and moaning to the point where it sounds like an orgasm. Watch out for his sleazy, skeevy cousin who lurks in the wet area and never works out at all.

The gym bunny - With all the hopping around that this tanned titan does—in his plunging tank top and tiny, tight shorts—it's amazing he has such a nice body. Maybe he works out at home.

THE AGE SWITCH

Many gay men—like the title character in Wilde's *Dorian Gray*—seem eerily ageless, and have the same or much better bodies in their thirties to forties than they ever did in their teens and twenties. How does this happen? Three significant reasons. First, the gay culture is somewhat (yeah, somewhat) obsessed with youth, beauty, and the body. When any of us can no longer classify ourselves as a "twinkie"—say around thirty (ha!)—and the "eyes" of the beholders are becoming scarce, we chart a course for the gym, knowing that we still have the power to keep one out of the three in our favor. Not *too* bad odds. Second, we *grew* these bodies to symbolically get back at all those schoolyard bullies and jocks (who, by this time, couldn't get off their coach-potato, post-peak butts to do anything about it anyway). Third, we have a different set of adult responsibilities then many of our heterosexual brethren—especially those who raise children. As adult males, this leaves us with playtime (and play money)—and we make good use of it. (If none of these seem to jibe with your handsome and hunky friend's situation, you might want to check for any portraits in his attic!)

THE DAILY ROUTINE

Some believe that all gay men languish in Mr Bubble for hours until pruny and pie-eyed. Sorry to disappoint, but simmering in our own soapy juices is not the preferred way for us to cleanse. Here, we like to stand up, shower, and be counted rather than lie down (and that is rare!). Admittedly, our regimen may also include that extra rinse and repeat, an unusual unguent or two, and special attention paid to nooks and crannies—which straight men puzzlingly seem to avoid. What is that all about?!

Nailed!

Few things are as welcome a sight as a pair of well-groomed hands. But here is where things can get "out" of hand:

- Getting a manicure in a nail salon.
- Filing or buffing his own nails.
- Getting a pedicure, anywhere.
- Staring at the nails with the back of hand extended flat in front of the face and fingers up. A *gaydar* classic.
- Nipping at the nails when nervous, and tapping the tips during same.
- *Too*-long nails (might be a drag queen).

TOM, DICK, AND HAPPILY HAIRY

Lest you think otherwise, *all* men are obsessed with their hair (most especially with any lack thereof). But when it comes to the coif and comb, there are ways to tell the gay hair do from any straight hair don't:

- Getting it cut at a *styling* salon
- A post-twenty something man getting blond or Pepe LePew/Cruella DeVil-inspired white highlights. Surprisingly, any all-over dye job—regardless of whether it is bottle blond or Jell-O green—is more funky than *fairy*-able fashioning
- Always opting for the latest style haircut (because it is a quick and easy way to say "club member" and usually cheaper than a new outfit)

"Parting" Ways

Gay "boys" usually have the safety net of formidable follicles; many gay "daddies" do not. Sensing the permanent loss of luxuriant locks, maturer men show savvy by buzzing what's left and growing a goatee or funky ("straighter") soul patch. (Note: Goatees used to be *gay*-stays—especially during their mid-nineties pop-peak—but straight men realized their sexy potential and things have become very hairy between us ever since.)

Splitting hairs?

For all men, shaving unruly chest hair (if it doesn't make us look like George Clooney) and back hair(!) is perfectly acceptable. Anywhere elsewhere—underarms, legs, groin, and buttocks (do you know how hard that is to do?)—even if he is a "straight" swimmer or bodybuilder, cuts things rather close. Gay-fave *hair* apparent? The delectable-directional "goody" trail (from navel to groin).

Gayest hairstyle?

Namely, "gay" haircuts do not exist. But some, like the "flip" (front or back) certainly turn our way. In addition, a "gay-ish" cut is usually distinguished by being neat and clean, especially at the nape of the neck (a *gay*-rogenous zone). Furthermore, even when it's messy ("bed-head" or "bird's nest") the look is deliberate. The *mane*-ly "gay" hair no-show? The mullet.

FACING FACTS

Gay men may pay more attention to their faces than straight men, but those extra moments do not mean we're dusting on powder or adding the blush of youth (but we do love a facial!). The extended effort now is so that we will be rewarded with ageless-looking skin later (and you know, it works!). Other "touchy" spots:

brows - a gay man will groom his brows of extralong Captain Kangaroo hairs. However, some pluck themselves into Joan Crawford. (Note: If a man is near-to-completely void of brow hairs, he may be the same potential drag queen from "Nailed" on page 79.)

bronzer - this *used* to be a classic gay sign: a pillow streaked with bronzer after a "hot" night in bed. Thankfully, with advances in self-tanners we can wake up streak-free.

lashes - no, not mascaraed, but frequently curled! A gay eye-opener.

lips - keeping them kissable is *man*-datory; how he does it can be very telling, indeed:

- Is stick balm swirled on a pursed kisser with a lipstick flourish?
- Does he dab and swirl a finger around pouted lips?
- Are either actions followed by an audible smack of newly waxed lips?

BODY ART

The gay body has gone from a simple temple into a muscled museum of art, and piercings were the first to use it as hanging gallery space (the right earlobe, his premier "hole" in the wall). Nowadays, *every* man might go under the needle. Still, some "pricks" are *gayer* than others:

the navel ring - symmetrical splendour, and so Janet
The Prince Albert - named for the well-endowed royal, who, so the rumour goes, had one himself

Recently, tattoos—lo of carnival dwellers and motorcyclists—have become *the* choice to adorn our frequently exposed canvases. Again, we share this passion with straight men, but "tats" are definitely insignias of the new gay masculine ideal. Thankfully, there are a few more "emblematic" than others:

sunburst/(downward) pointing arrow - just above his buttocks
rose/star/cute baby animal - on his right or left butt cheek
latticework/vine/chain pattern - across his upper right (bottom) or left (top) arm, between the deltoid and biceps

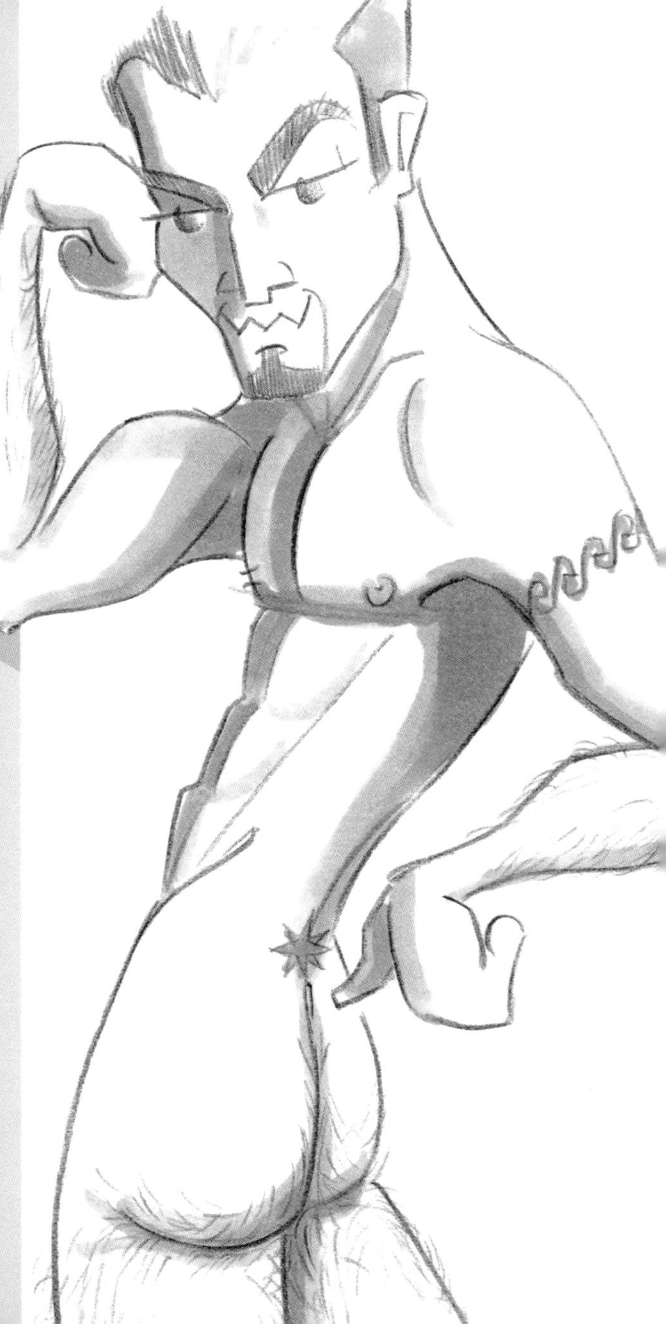

gaywear

For a very long time, gay men have used modes of dressing as a major means of identification to one another (which is safer and more esoteric than grabbing at a crotch, but not nearly as much fun!). Inclusion into the "brotherhood" of similarly dressed helped dispel feelings of separation and anxiety, and this made it an important part of gay life. But now maybe too important. While he expects scrutiny of his home and occupation for signs of success or failure, he believes clothes are what really make the gay man. This all came about because gay men are so inextricably sewn up with the "business and commerce" of fashion; it is something of a duty for us to dress well, or at least "try it on." (Not only that, we have to look as good in our clothes as we do out of them!) Further, motives seem to have shifted from those of pure acceptance and recognition into use by a class system for distinguishing the homosexual haves from the have-nots. Nevertheless, many gay men do have a marvelous sense of style—which they could only have been born with—and the world is sartorially more splendid because they were. Now if we can just do something about the wanting wardrobes of those who weren't.

GAY, NOT GAY?

Fashion runs *hot* or *cold*, *in* or *out*; it can also be *gay* or *straight*. But when is fashion gay and when is it not? Most of the time *hot* looks are synonymous with being gay because we designed, marketed, or purchased them first. However, once they are accepted by the mainstream you will notice our hasty departure, and the look becomes *cold*, *out*, or *straight*.

Who Wants to be a Macho Man?

Lately, gay men are quicker to adapt looks that harden (masculinize) his *mien* (example: facial hair) and are slower, understandably, with those that may soften (feminize) his appearance. Ironically, straight men seem to be doing the exact opposite. Two examples—showing the waistbands of underwear and wearing quarter crew sport socks—have extreme gay connotations, but have been wholly enfolded into the hetero male "closet." Hmmm.

Popped-Seam Quiz

What does "on the bias" mean? A surprising number of gay men should *ease*-ily be able to answer that question. However, to assume that all of us could might be a "stretch." For the answer, see page 132.

The Name Game

How does one play this popular gay parlour game? Easy. All it takes is for a "friend" to blurt out the name of any designer hoping it will match the label in the back of your shirt, tie, or inside your suit or shoe. If right, he wins—guess what?!—nothing except, hopefully, the admiration of those who believe knowing the "current" width of a tie or the toe shape of a shoe can change the world. Just think, no silly plastic pieces to watch over and no one has to play banker! Variations of this game can be played in areas of film, books, and music. *Beaucoup* fun for everyone!

The Fast-Slow Change Artist

It takes a man (straight or gay) no longer than one-millionth of a second to shuck both his pants and underwear down to his socks—if he has incentive (and it doesn't take much!). But varying the speed of exposure or closure takes true gay aptitude. The best place for viewing and perfecting this is a locker room. While dressing, one may be offered a tantalizing flash-in-the-pants moment; see a guy linger teasingly naked; or be greeted on the street by the same person, now fully clothed, even though *you* walked out first. Truly amazing!

Six Words to Describe Gay Clothes

shorter • ***tighter***
sleeker • ***refined***
revealing • ***exclusive***

Things That *Drag* Him "Out of the Closet"

- multiples of same items in different colors: sweaters, swimsuits, and sunglasses
- guides to dressing better
- clothes made of *only* the finest quality fabrics (cashmere, vicuna, silks), spandex blends, and *imported* polyesters
- shoe trees and shoe bags
- padded hangers (no wire hangers, ever! Which is from what film? See page 132.)
- Any item with a touch (or torrent) of sparkle

Making a Show of It

In and of itself, a single piece of clothing is often not enough to place it in gay territory. Color can push it over the border. Pastels—any color with a large amount of white added—is the gayest range in the rainbow. But surprisingly, bright colors—from fire-engine red to cobalt blue—tend more toward the funky than the fairyland edge of the fashion palette.

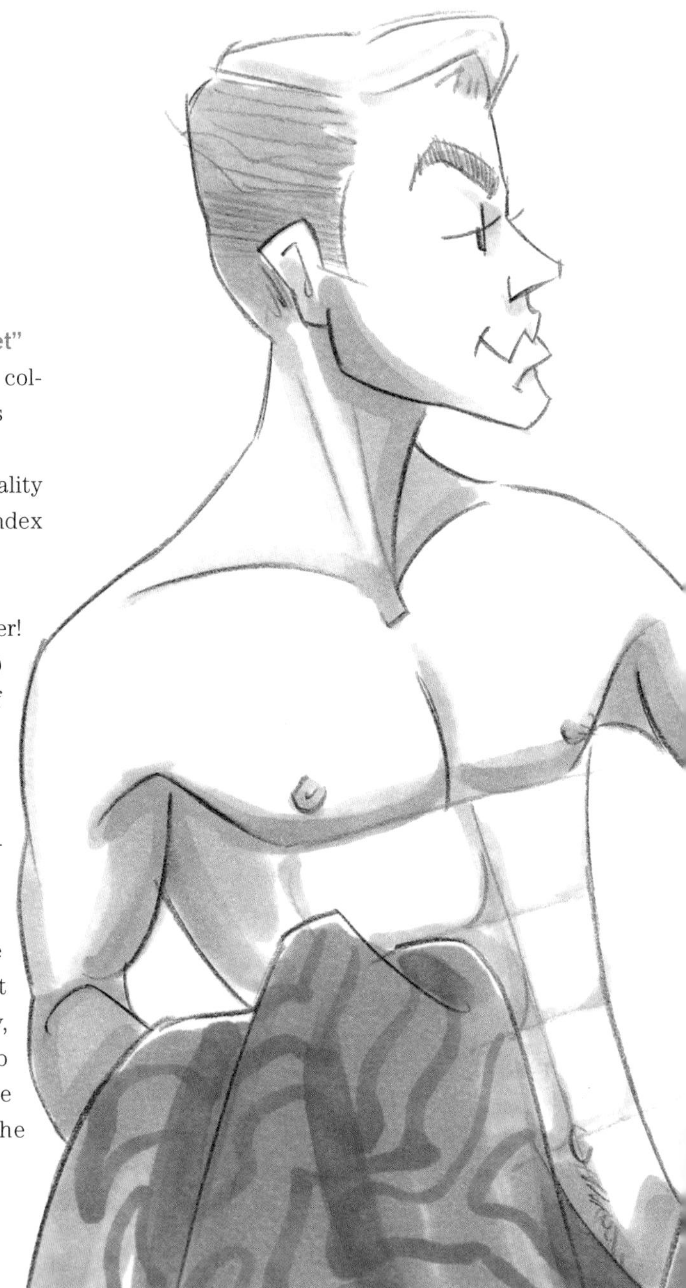

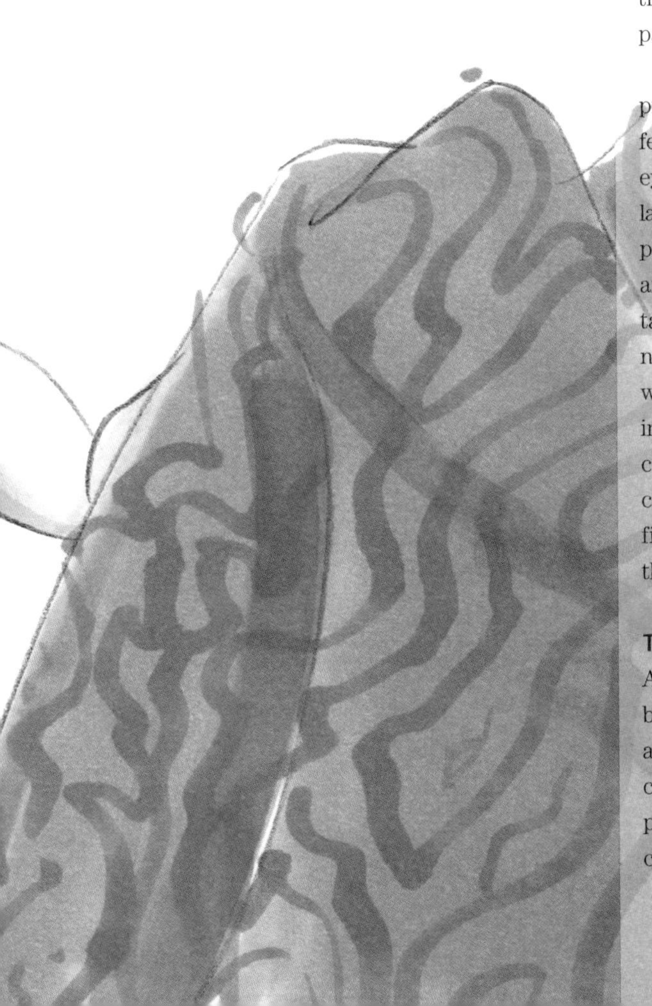

Prints are another way clothes pledge their allegiance to one side or the other. But they, too, divide themselves between both "camps." Zebra stripes are not the same gay bull's-eye as the festive floral, and a paisley tie is not near as "queer" as when the same pattern appears on a shirt.

However, scholarship of "shade" lore is a proficiently gay sign. Only "he" knows the difference in appearance—which to the straight eye may not seem as life-threateningly similar—between hot pink, magenta, and fuchsia; plum, burgundy, and wine; egg-shell, cream, and ivory. He will also understand the important, goes-with-everything versatility of the neutrals: mauve, taupe, and beige; and the wardrobe extendability factor of color matching, color coordinating, and monochromatic colors. However, maybe most striking is his comprehension of the fact that khaki was first a Hindi name for dust-colored cloth, then a fashion staple. Genius!

The Color Lavender

Although pink is the color most assumed to be the "gayest" (triangles, golf pro attire, and whatnot), lavender, because of its delicate mixing of baby blue (for boys) *with* pink (for girls), is actually the official queer color (and shade of choice for *Gaydar*).

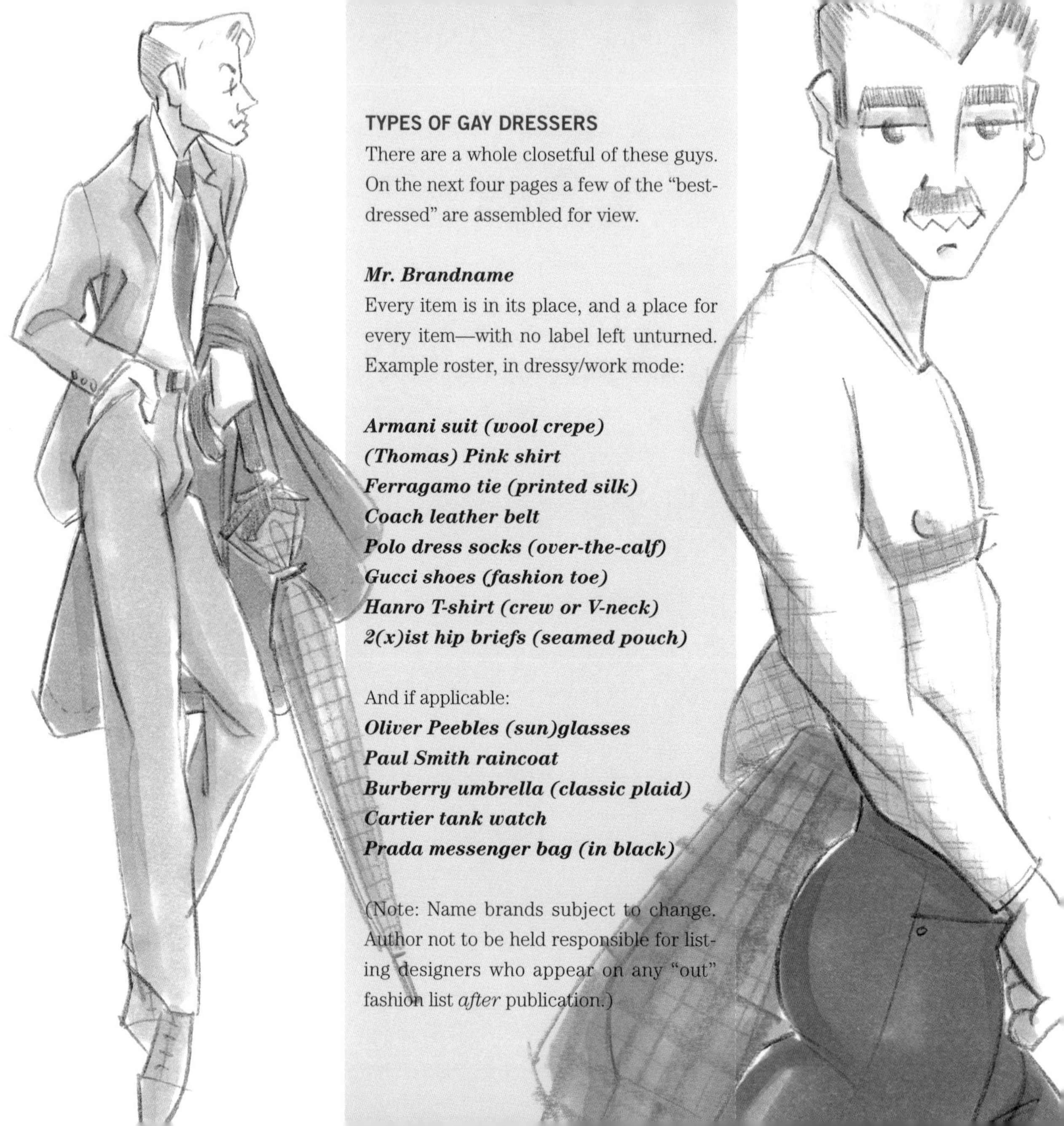

TYPES OF GAY DRESSERS

There are a whole closetful of these guys. On the next four pages a few of the "best-dressed" are assembled for view.

Mr. Brandname

Every item is in its place, and a place for every item—with no label left unturned. Example roster, in dressy/work mode:

Armani suit (wool crepe)
(Thomas) Pink shirt
Ferragamo tie (printed silk)
Coach leather belt
Polo dress socks (over-the-calf)
Gucci shoes (fashion toe)
Hanro T-shirt (crew or V-neck)
2(x)ist hip briefs (seamed pouch)

And if applicable:
Oliver Peebles (sun)glasses
Paul Smith raincoat
Burberry umbrella (classic plaid)
Cartier tank watch
Prada messenger bag (in black)

(Note: Name brands subject to change. Author not to be held responsible for listing designers who appear on any "out" fashion list *after* publication.)

The Clone

Upon his mid-1970s arrival, this hairy-chested, crew-cut styled, handlebar mustachioed man was so pervasive he was originally coined the "gay clone." In plaid flannel shirt, exposed waffle-weave longjohns, and well-worn button-front jeans, "daddy" was obviously mimicking the straight outdoorsman icon—all the way down to his red-striped grey sweatsocks and scruffy construction boots. (*Mucho* seventies actor Sam Elliott.) "He" exists in mutated form today: less hirsute and clothed, but more buff, and part of that beefy battalion commonly referred to as the "circuit boys."

Mr T.O.C. (Total Outfit Coordination)

Cousin to Mr Brandname. However, Mr T.O.C.'s clothes usually appear in either one color (usually black, and *most* slimming), monochromatically (taupes, khakis, etc.), or color coordinated, such as the very gay matching of, say, purple socks with a purple tie, or a beige shirt with similarly toned men's hosiery (still gay, but not as in-your-face).

Mr Young Republican

Often too conservative for his own gay good—is he straight?—this collegiate *queer*-leader is still the ultimate preppy pinup boy.

The Homeboy

In his anti-*body* clothes—baggy jeans, oversized sweatshirts, etc.—Mr Homeboy *appears* the least gay. Still, many gay men find his look appealing and even include adjunct "street" dialogue in their recreation. But no matter how streetwise, we often go one step too far. Whether it's being *too* pulled together—or that dainty pedicure!—you'll find an Achilles' heel that'll bring him down to his knees.

The Hustler

The pieces of this hunk's limited wardrobe include three most important staples of a gay man's wardrobe: tight white T-shirt, jeans with provocative "wearmarks" and "tears," and black leather jacket.

The Party Boy

Like the earth's surface, only thirty percent of this stud's body is covered, leaving seventy percent exposed, sweat-coated skin. (Here, less leaves definitely more for the viewer to enjoy!) Regardless, even the skimpiest piece of Dolce & Gabbana comes with a hefty price tag, so don't expect any bargains.

The Fop

The dandiest of all dressers, and an obvious gay target: his polka-dot bow ties make him way too easy to spot. However, this skinny minikin is protected by the force field supplied by his bright, striped shirts and loud plaid pants, which keep people at a safe, blinded distance. Cousin? The Peacock (see page 98).

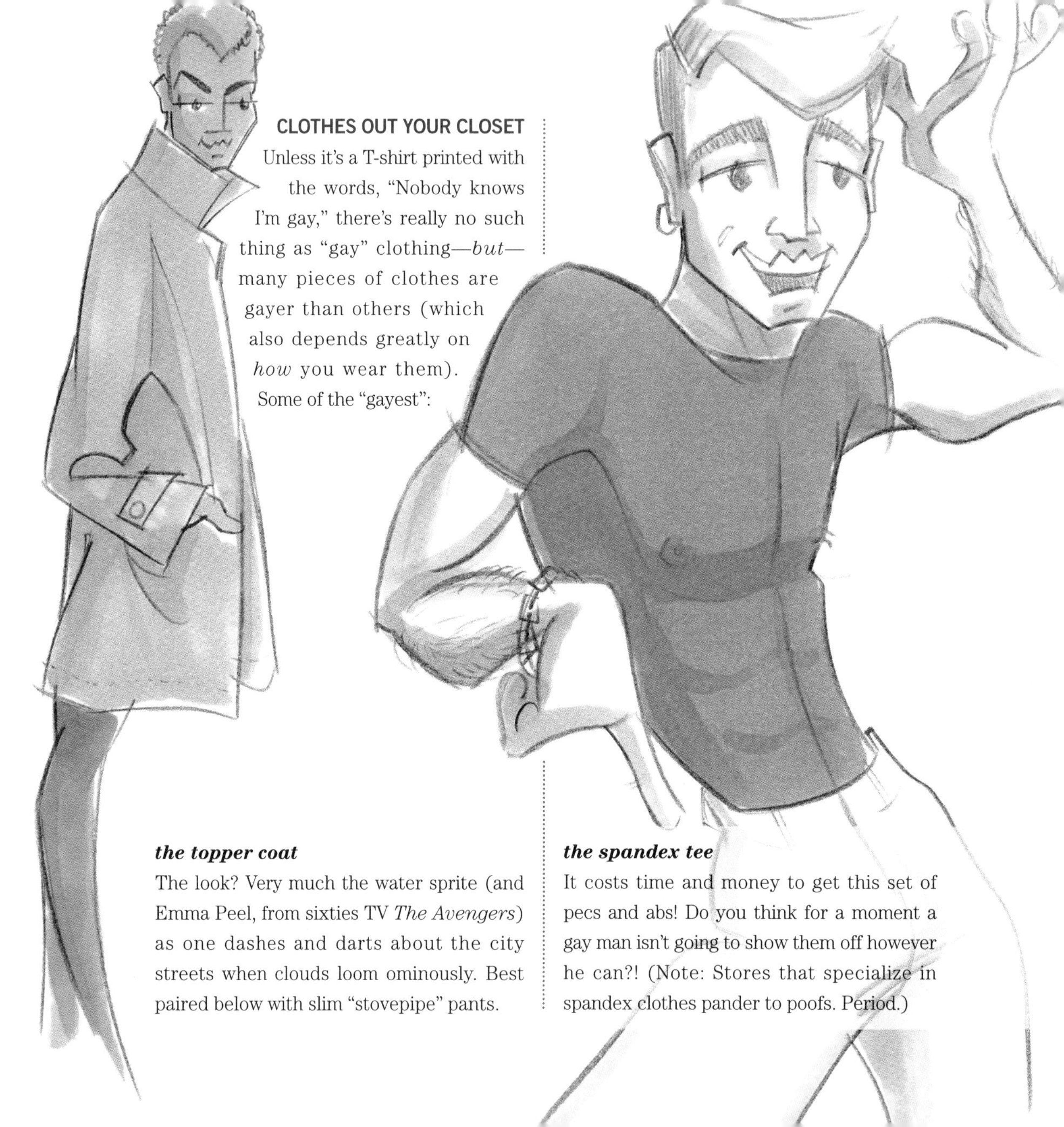

CLOTHES OUT YOUR CLOSET

Unless it's a T-shirt printed with the words, "Nobody knows I'm gay," there's really no such thing as "gay" clothing—*but*—many pieces of clothes are gayer than others (which also depends greatly on *how* you wear them). Some of the "gayest":

the topper coat

The look? Very much the water sprite (and Emma Peel, from sixties TV *The Avengers*) as one dashes and darts about the city streets when clouds loom ominously. Best paired below with slim "stovepipe" pants.

the spandex tee

It costs time and money to get this set of pecs and abs! Do you think for a moment a gay man isn't going to show them off however he can?! (Note: Stores that specialize in spandex clothes pander to poofs. Period.)

the 4-button suit

Very Savile Row, and most slenderizing when tailored in divinely drapable wool crepe. Should not be worn if one expects to do anything more strenuous than posing in front of a mirror. Perfection with a walking stick.

the cardigan sweater

Thanks to manly men like Mister Rogers, how could you not help but realize the potentially fey quality of this fashion staple. Sure they're comfy-cozy, but is that a feeling desirous of a straight man?

Bottoms Are Tops!

What a gay man wears below the waist can make his sexual preference as obvious as if he kept his pants off all the time. But leaving his stick shift in high gear like that is not terribly practical (unless he's a porn star). Here are two combos that should have him *not* pant-ing:

- denim cutoff (very short) shorts, construction boots, casually laced, and the magic touch of a scrunched-down boot sock. Not seen: a white, but worn, jockstrap. *Voilà!* instant sissy signature outfit.
- White designer-brand seamed-pouch hip briefs and white sweatsocks. (Note: thongs can be *too* queer—even for us—unless we're dancers or looking to reduce visible outside lines. Yes, we do worry about that.)

Two very telling "waisted" *gay*-dicators: If the size (up to 36, past that is *too* big) is numerically smaller than his age; and if he tucks his shirt into his underwear (a "trick" he could only have learned from his days dressing models).

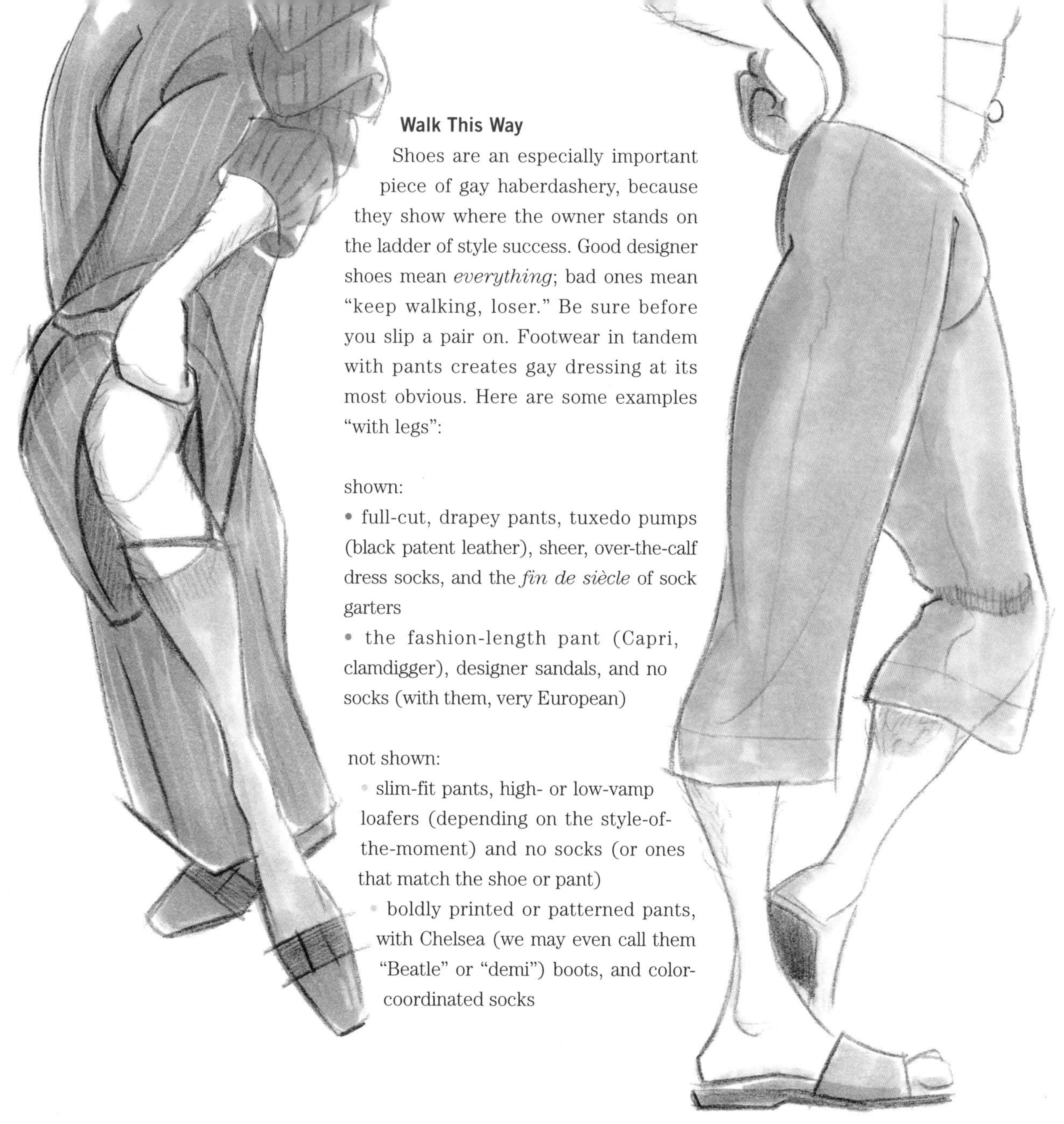

Walk This Way

Shoes are an especially important piece of gay haberdashery, because they show where the owner stands on the ladder of style success. Good designer shoes mean *everything*; bad ones mean "keep walking, loser." Be sure before you slip a pair on. Footwear in tandem with pants creates gay dressing at its most obvious. Here are some examples "with legs":

shown:

- full-cut, drapey pants, tuxedo pumps (black patent leather), sheer, over-the-calf dress socks, and the *fin de siècle* of sock garters
- the fashion-length pant (Capri, clamdigger), designer sandals, and no socks (with them, very European)

not shown:

- slim-fit pants, high- or low-vamp loafers (depending on the style-of-the-moment) and no socks (or ones that match the shoe or pant)
- boldly printed or patterned pants, with Chelsea (we may even call them "Beatle" or "demi") boots, and color-coordinated socks

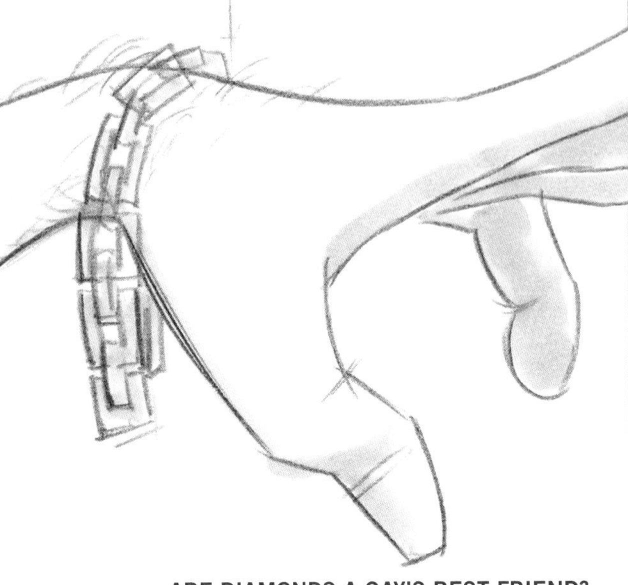

ARE DIAMONDS A GAY'S BEST FRIEND?

Maybe, but only if he's past forty (what film is that thought lifted from? see page 132). Until then he will have to suffer through with silver (or platinum) bracelets and one had better hope *not* gold (a bit *recherché, n'est-ce pas?* another film; see page 132). In fact, all types of *arm*ature have become quite popular with gay men, from the ubiquitous designer links to the handy leather money holder (so perfect when wearing rubber pants without pockets). Then there is the watch. Which is still—along with his shoes (and ties if applicable)—the way a gay man can gauge another's date- and mate-ability. The better the watch; the better the chances it could be left behind on your nightstand.

THE *GAI*-MENTS OF DRESSING WELL

In the same way that a gay man may use etiquette to bespeak his place in proper society, he will uphold certain standards of dressing to claim some cultural class. If the occasion calls for black tie, you can be sure his will be the blackest. His mahogany armoire will contain many splendid specimens of this fading finery:

- short, one-button white kid leather gloves
- self-tied black silk bow tie
- diamond or jet shirt studs
- stone-set (diamond, ruby) cufflinks
- white, silk faille, fringed scarf
- an assortment of printed Hermès silk cravats, for when the fete is not formal. (Basically, the gay man's version of a woman's scarf, for tying around his neck.)
- pocket watch and fob
- tie-matching kerchiefs for breast pocket
- (those homo-sexy) sock garters
- lapel and tie pins
- collar bars and permanent collar stays

*Out*side his armoire:

- A red rose *boutonniere*

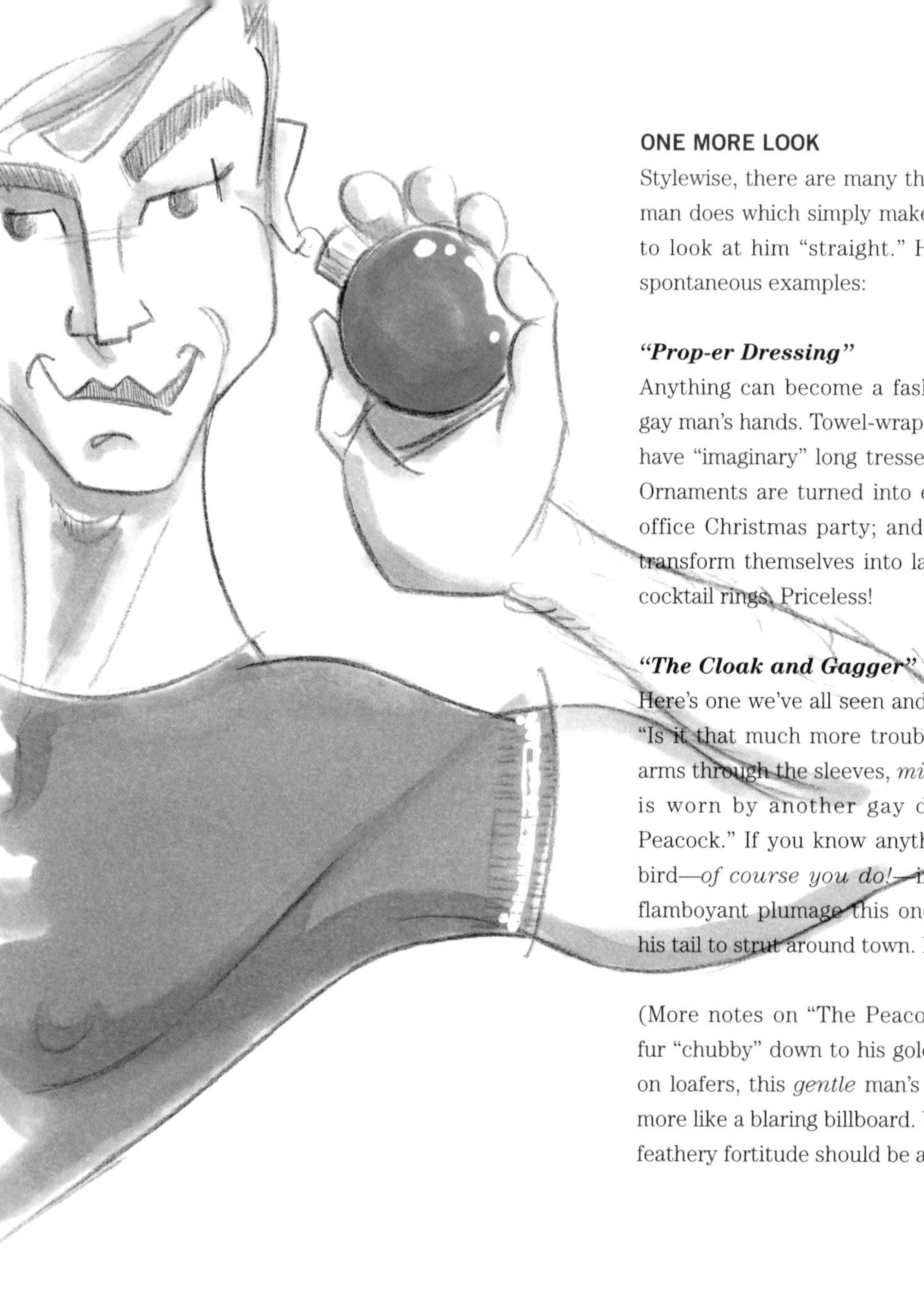

ONE MORE LOOK

Stylewise, there are many things that a gay man does which simply make it *impossible* to look at him "straight." Here are three spontaneous examples:

"Prop-er Dressing"

Anything can become a fashion prop in a gay man's hands. Towel-wrapped heads now have "imaginary" long tresses to play with; Ornaments are turned into earrings at the office Christmas party; and paperweights transform themselves into large, "Zsa Zsa" cocktail rings. Priceless!

"The Cloak and Gagger"

Here's one we've all seen and then thought, "Is it that much more trouble to put your arms through the sleeves, *missy?*" The look is worn by another gay dresser, "The Peacock." If you know anything about the bird—*of course you do!*—imagine all the flamboyant plumage this one can stick on his tail to strut around town. Fabulous!

(More notes on "The Peacock:" From his fur "chubby" down to his gold metallic slip-on loafers, this *gentle* man's calling card is more like a blaring billboard. Yet his fearless feathery fortitude should be applauded.)

"A Mink Stolen Moment"

The scene: a jacket drops off the shoulders and is clutched—along with any personal items (agendas, books, bags) around his mid-section in an ensnaring *gaydar* classic move—just like the mink stole worn by a movie starlet at a Grauman's Chinese Theatre premiere. Bravo!

gaysport

Gay men and sports? Despite what you may have heard we do engage in physical activity *outside* of the bedroom. Whether we excelled at sports in school or buffed up afterwards to hit the tarmac, some of us are quite good athletes and can certainly hold our own against all comers. Of course, there are some sports more gay-inclined than others. Not surprisingly, most of these place enormous emphasis on the bulging beauty of the male form and require wearing tight, body-revealing uniforms. But you certainly don't have to be gay to play. In any event, even the most notoriously straight games—football, baseball, hockey—have their gay moments (*ahem,* butt grabbing), though team members of all sports vigorously deny *any* questionable goings on. Additionally, as was the case with occupations, to name a sport "gay" does not mean straight men can not share in the fun or to underplay their participation (when it occurs). Nor should it be taken as an indication that being a "gay" sport means it is a less physically strenuous undertaking. We sweat as much as you, but only do a much better job of cleaning up after the game.

Three Sports We *Wish* Were Gay

water polo • rugby • soccer

Figure Skating

Oh, I don't know, it could just be me projecting. But a sport devoted almost exclusively to spinning around on one foot to the background strains of classical or, more likely, show music; lifting, kicking, twirling, and holding your legs higher than your *derrière;* extending your arms, hands, and fingertips to create the longest, cleanest line; while wearing chest-baring tops that accentuate movement and skintight bottoms to emphasize that same fabulous prized ass, and smiling as much as possible over your Vaseline-coated teeth, just seems to scream "ice queen." But again, it could just be me. (Note: Speed skating is not really a gay-friendly sport, but you won't have to look far to find a gay man riveted to his TV set when one of these thigh masters comes onscreen.)

Ladies' Nite?

Every four years, on the night of the Olympic finals for ladies' figure skating, a gay man will display much of the same fervor he reserves for the yearly Academy Awards. He will tune in days earlier to the men's finals, but only to check out who's cute, who has the best butt, and which poor thing wore the most ridiculous outfit.

Wrestling

In the Land of Straight Male Denial you can delude yourself into thinking that you are witnessing two Herculean he-men battling it out for the hand of some extremely buxom she-maiden (or some gaudily decorated championship belt). However from *this* vantage point, things look a little twisted, *sister*. Look at all those sweaty, "role-playing" men, grabbing at each other's crotch, and then using their massive thighs to squeeze the air out of a teeny-tiny spandex-clad opponent. What gives? Certainly not those headlocks! And have you really seen what little some of these guys wear?!

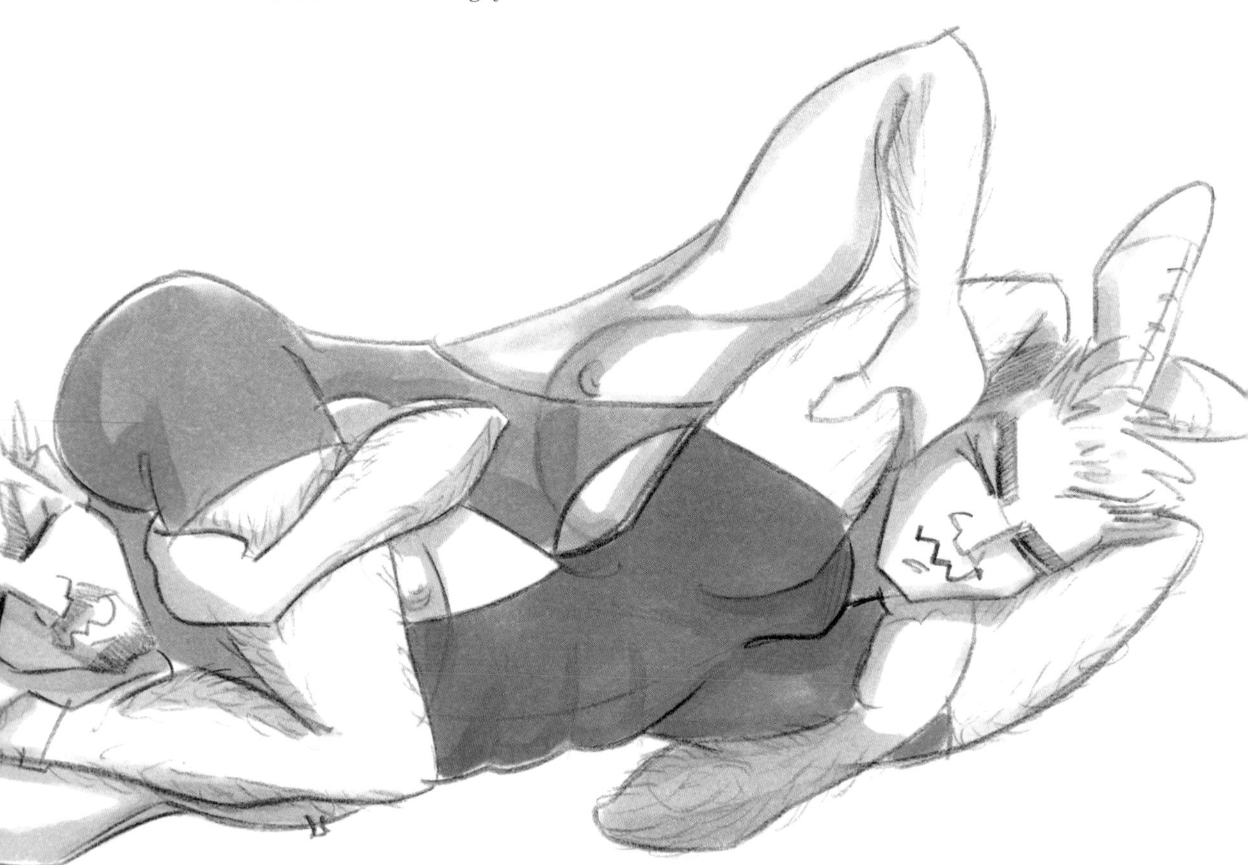

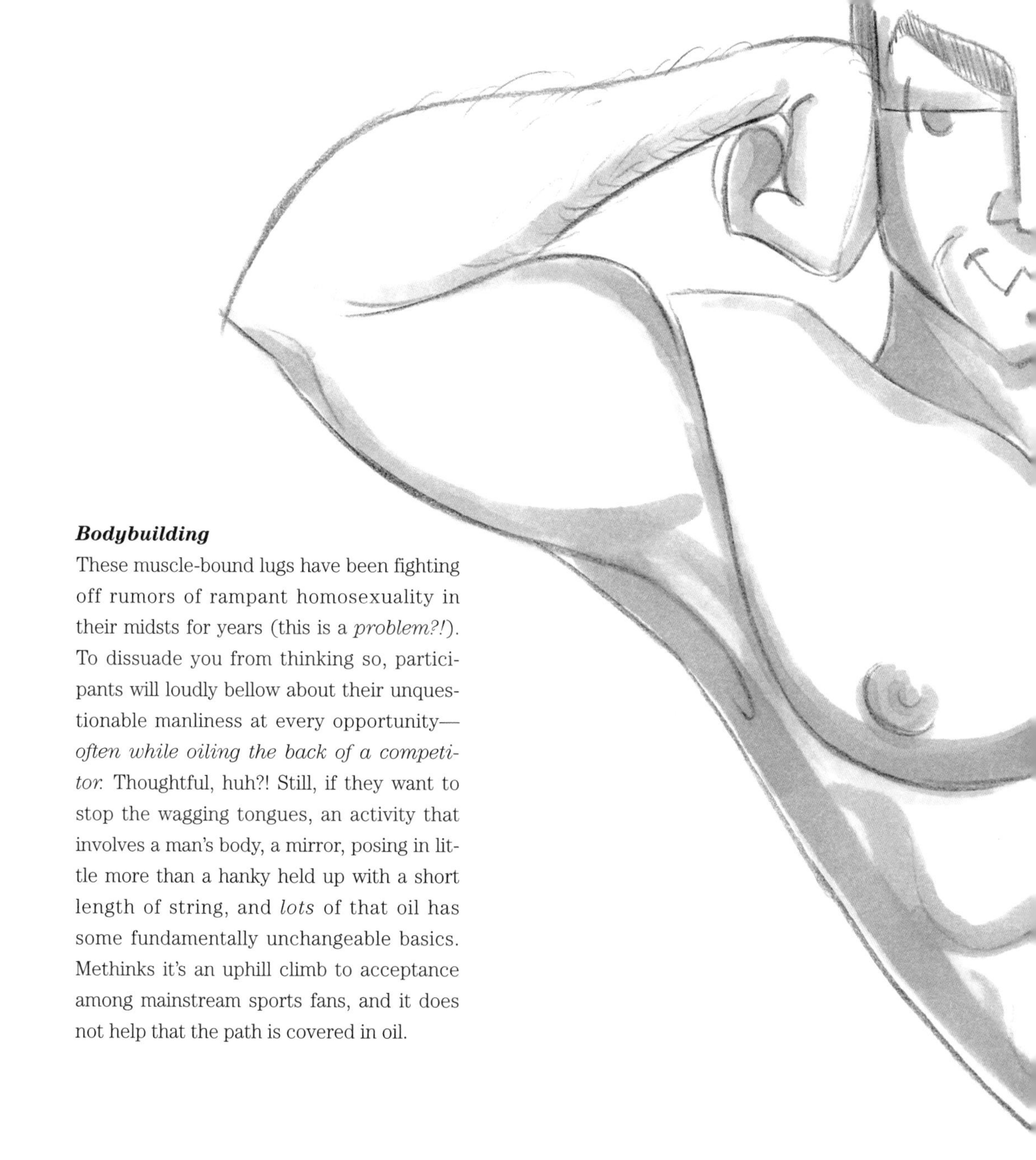

Bodybuilding

These muscle-bound lugs have been fighting off rumors of rampant homosexuality in their midsts for years (this is a *problem?!*). To dissuade you from thinking so, participants will loudly bellow about their unquestionable manliness at every opportunity—*often while oiling the back of a competitor.* Thoughtful, huh?! Still, if they want to stop the wagging tongues, an activity that involves a man's body, a mirror, posing in little more than a hanky held up with a short length of string, and *lots* of that oil has some fundamentally unchangeable basics. Methinks it's an uphill climb to acceptance among mainstream sports fans, and it does not help that the path is covered in oil.

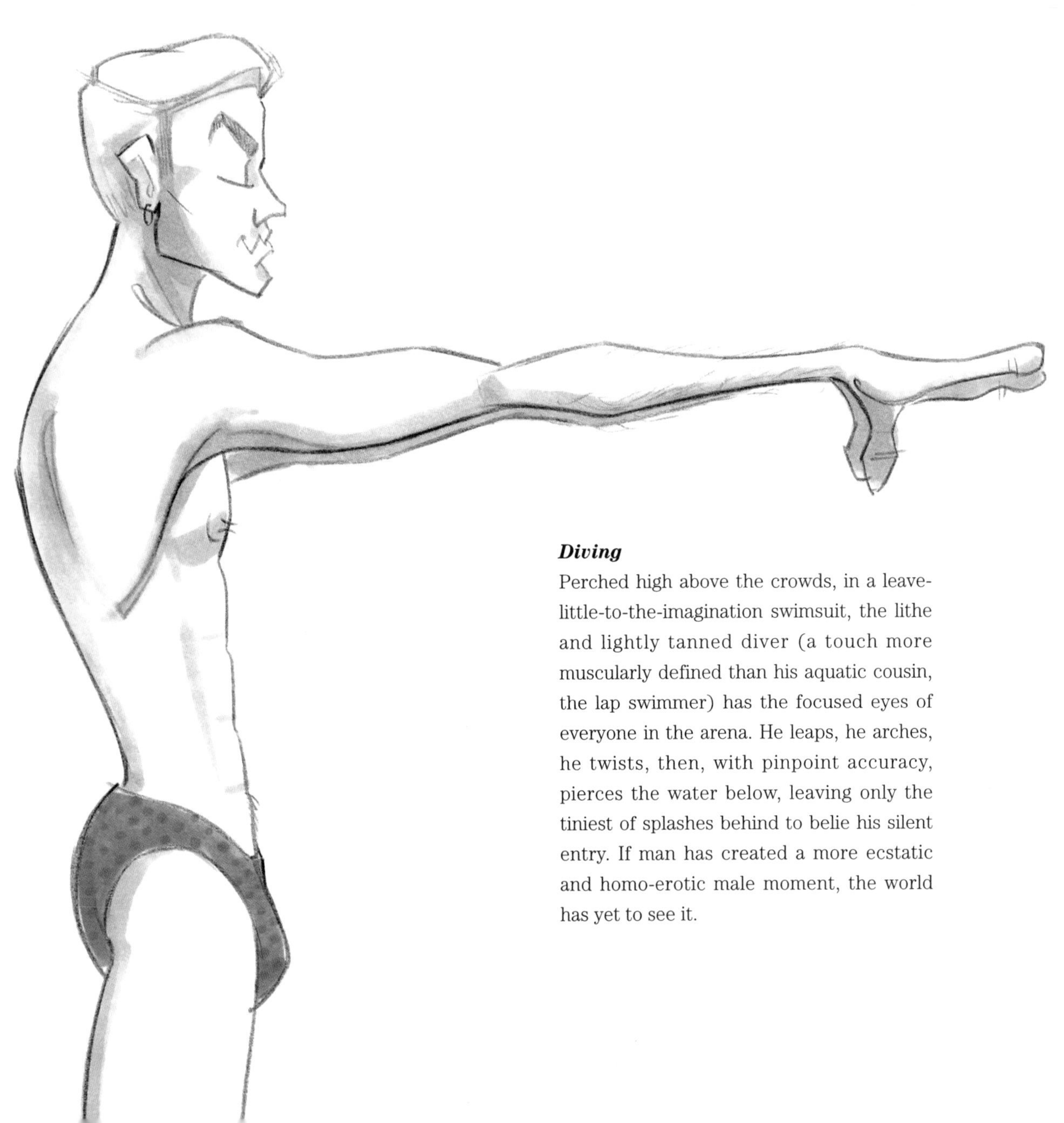

Diving

Perched high above the crowds, in a leave-little-to-the-imagination swimsuit, the lithe and lightly tanned diver (a touch more muscularly defined than his aquatic cousin, the lap swimmer) has the focused eyes of everyone in the arena. He leaps, he arches, he twists, then, with pinpoint accuracy, pierces the water below, leaving only the tiniest of splashes behind to belie his silent entry. If man has created a more ecstatic and homo-erotic male moment, the world has yet to see it.

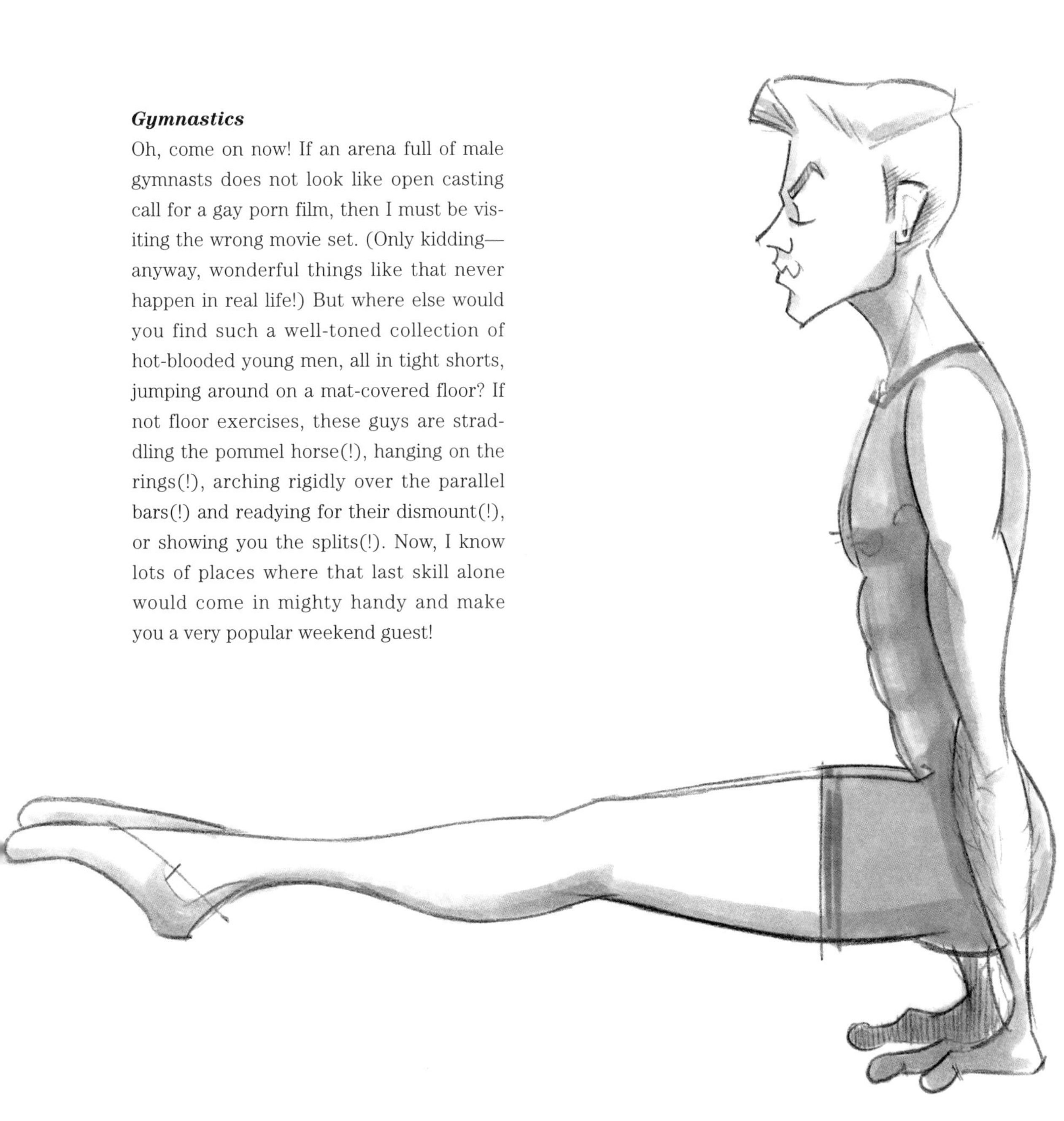

Gymnastics

Oh, come on now! If an arena full of male gymnasts does not look like open casting call for a gay porn film, then I must be visiting the wrong movie set. (Only kidding—anyway, wonderful things like that never happen in real life!) But where else would you find such a well-toned collection of hot-blooded young men, all in tight shorts, jumping around on a mat-covered floor? If not floor exercises, these guys are straddling the pommel horse(!), hanging on the rings(!), arching rigidly over the parallel bars(!) and readying for their dismount(!), or showing you the splits(!). Now, I know lots of places where that last skill alone would come in mighty handy and make you a very popular weekend guest!

Lugeing

It wouldn't be fair to consider this a "gay" sport on the same ice as figure skating, but its abundance of *super* hot men (I mean have you *seen* these guys?!) should melt away any doubts about its continued *gay*-doration. The "set-up:" a pair of almost impossibly beautiful and built men, in stretchy full-body suits (just like a one-piece Speedo, and you know how crazy gay men are for those!), lying atop one another on the smallest sliverlike sled. The larger man is on the bottom; the smaller, resting his head upon his partner's chest area, is cradled between the other's legs. Whoa! To get anything more *into* this, you'd need some lubricant!

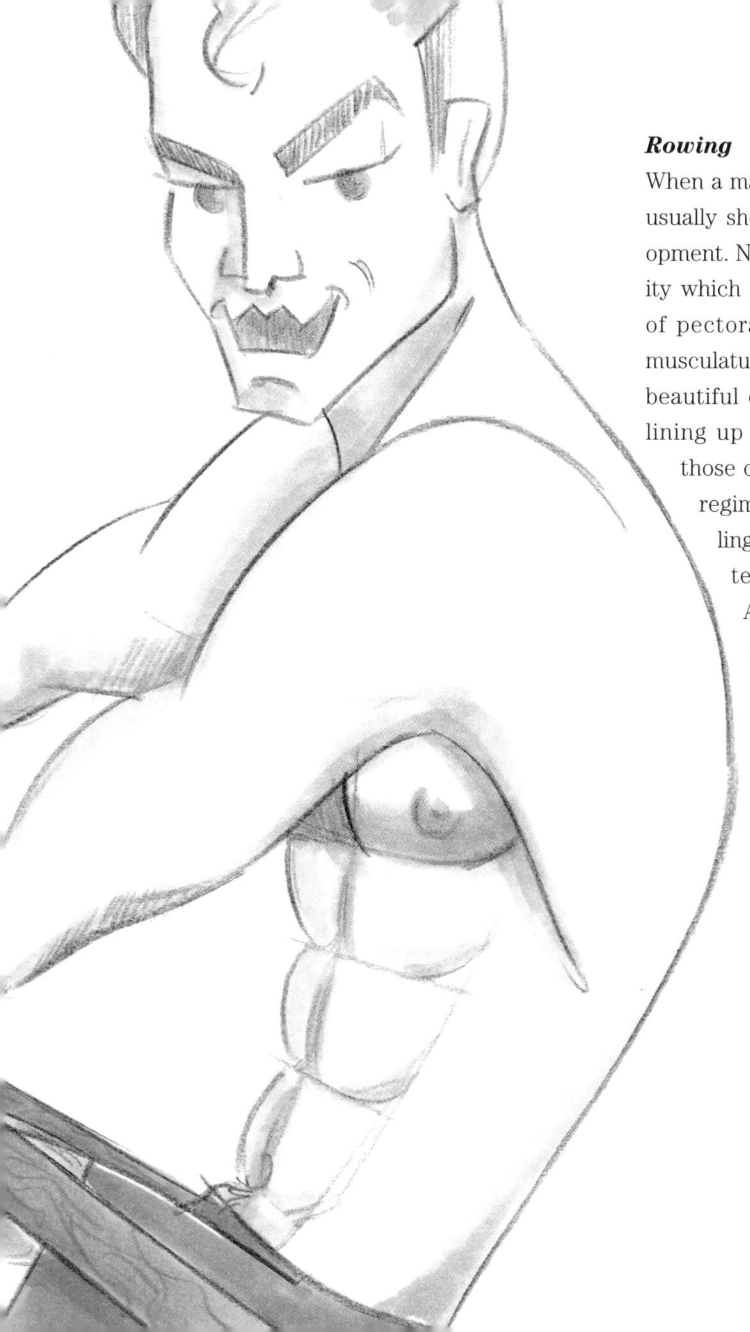

Rowing

When a man exercises, his upper body area usually shows the fastest amount of development. Needless to say, any sporting activity which can further aid in the quick gain of pectoral, deltoid, biceps, and triceps musculature (and we gay men do *so* love a beautiful chest and arms) will have them lining up along the shore, ready to grab those oars! Rowing is also an *extremely* regimented sport, which any controlling, body-obsessed homosexual will tell you is impossible not to like. And, as if that weren't enough, you have that *hunky* helmsman to keep your stroking precise and orderly. Thank goodness we're out on the water where a cool breeze can keep us from passing out at the "hot" thought of it all.

In-line skating

Of the millions who have found physical nirvana in blading, you will find an overwhelming abundance of happy homosexuals. Why?

- Nothing defines calf, thigh, and those important butt muscles quicker than a few laps around the park.
- You can incorporate music into your workout, allowing one to create a choreographed personal masterpiece, worthy of an MTV heavy-rotation video.
- You work up a sweat that just begs for you to strip—affording a glorious glimpse at your glistening pectoral muscles—which many gay men jump at the chance to do.
- You're instantly three inches taller!

Cycling

This speedy sport—with its aerodynamic cycles; tight, cap-sleeved tops festooned with brightly colored emblems; spandex shorts with padding in the buttocks; and jaunty little shoes to match—is right up our alley (but those helmets are another story!). And any sport featuring a roiling army of pedal-pumping men on wheels—with those lean, mean thighs—is definitely headed in the right (or would that be "left?") direction.

gayplay

What does a gay man do when he is not working, working out, sleeping, or sleeping around? In this final section, a few answers.

TALK, TALK, TALK (GOSSIPING)
Growing up, many gay youths were one (if not all three) of these types of boy:

shy and introverted
bright and talented
little nonstop chatterboxes

Does this next statement sound familiar? "Name of boy is a very smart child, but he has the problem of talking with neighbors in class." I thought it would. This loose-lipped love affair does not end in childhood. Grown gay men adore whiling away the hours conferring about the flowers; harmless so long as you remember to pay the rent. However, if we don't hold back our tongues now and then, we run the risk of morphing into full-blown gossiping gay queens. This is not really a bad way to pass on valuable and time-sensitive information—like the latest fashion *faux pas* and sexploits of closeted male stars—but too many of us never know when to stop. Well, "you know how bitchy fags can be." (What film and character? see page 132.)

"I hear he's trying to lose weight!"

"'She's' such a mess!"

"Did you see that outfit?"

"Where did you dig him up?"

TELL US HOW IT REALLY IS (CRITIQUING)

No matter how small or large, if a thing exists in this world a gay man has an opinion about it. Though this comment comes from a place of great compassion and understanding of the subject it may sound like negative criticism—as opposed to positive reinforcement—but hearing it is for your own good. (*Poor thing, obviously doesn't know any better.*) Alteration in behavior on your part isn't really necessary—(*you wouldn't do it right, anyway*)—but I just couldn't rest knowing I hadn't given you my thoughts. (*Ho-hum. As if it will do any good.*) Promise me you'll think about what I've said? Good, let's continue this later.

By the way, if it hasn't already occurred to you, *Gaydar* is a book full of one gay man's droll diatribe on one subject. "The mind reels!" (What movie, character, and actress? See page 132.)

Best Served Cold?

Gossip is a tasty but tart *dish* filled with spicy *attitude*, juicy bits of *scandale,* and opinions *à la mode*. A meal of this may make you feel full, but in an hour you'll be hungry again. Gay men already have some empty calorie items on their plates. Avoid a steady diet of this *entrée* if you can. If you can't, *sugar,* come sit by me.

"I could barely sit through it!"

"I certainly wouldn't do it that way!"

"I really couldn't care less, but if you want my opinion . . ."

GAY-LOPING GOURMETS (DINING)

The same bill of fare which promises all gay men are a mix of model mannequin, esteemable aesthete, and cinematic connoiseur must surely include gargantuan gastronome. However, in reality, too many of us cookies crumble when we're in the kitchen. Fortunately, dining out saves the day with an equally important (if not more so) gay pastime than cooking: restaurant and meal recommendations. Why? Without question, gay men love telling people where to go for the ultimate dining experience and what exquisitely prepared courses to order when they do. *Bon appétit!*

What's Cooking?

Very questionable food items on the gay menu:

coffee	***bottled water***
leafy greens	***energy bars***
cigarettes	***chewing gum***
Absolut	***Ecstasy***

A *Happy* Meal?

In public, who is the gay or straight diner? Imagine this scenario: two great-looking, perfectly dressed men together in a very nice restaurant. Impeccable table manners. Harmless flirting with male waiter. An order of bottled water (no tap), a salad (containing the bitter greens: endive and arugula), grilled salmon, a crisp chardonnay (to go with the fish), and *no* dessert. Full twenty-percent tip. Must I peel the banana further? Amusingly, straight men think they can avoid suspicions of "coupling" by bringing a third or fourth male along for the ride. Tut, tut, boys! Hasn't anyone told them the more men the *Mary*-er?!

MR. BUTTERFLY (SOCIALIZING)

Some enchanted evening, you may see this beautiful stranger across a crowded room. Somehow you know you will see him again—and again. How you can spot him before he spots you:

- Stands only under light that casts flattering shadows across face and body.
- Poses in a completely sexualized (though subliminal) manner that shows off a "perkier-than-yours" butt at the same time forcing his "I-dare-you-to-stare" crotch outward
- Stares discreetly at all men in the room to size up the competition (if he thinks he has any), and keep his own *gaydar* in working order.
- Drinks the season's "hot" cocktail (prettily colored, fruit-flavored, and a touch too sweet to the taste).
- Tosses off witty asides about the right people, right places, and right parties.

Two *queer* quaffers:

"The sweetheart sipper"

Drinker forms "inverted" heart shape by bending elbows and clutching hands around tumbler-sized drink (with straw). Facial expressions limited to squinting.

"The gyrated libator"

Drinker is twisted perilously at waist, with one hand (extended with *gaydar* classic of "hovering pinkie) holding drink in longstemmed glass. The other hand may be clasping a slim cigarette "scissors" style, or have thumb hooked inside waistband, near the zipper, coaxing your *gay*ze in the direction of his crotch.

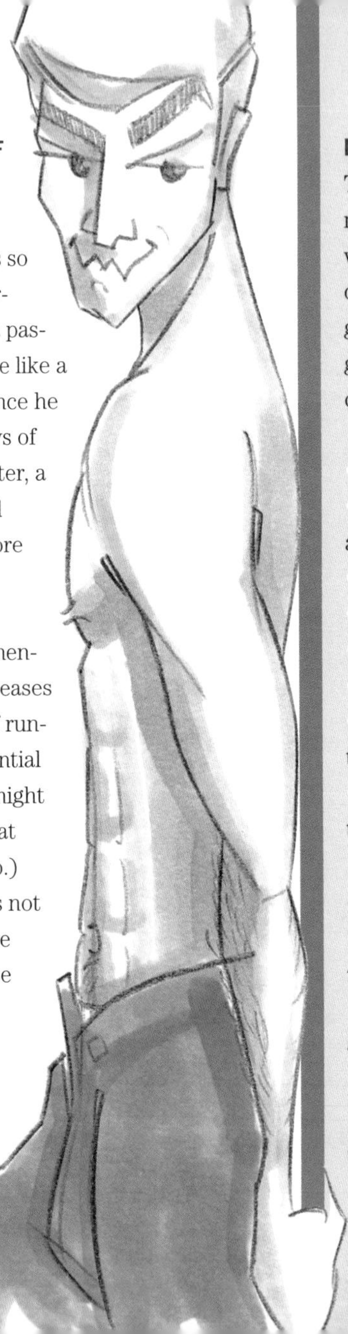

THE LOOK OF "LOVE?" (CRUISING)

This activity is so common it surpasses being a pastime—it's more like a gay alltime. Once he learns the ways of the cruisemaster, a gay man could potentially score whenever he wants. (This "autocruise" mentality also increases his chances of running into potential and past one-night stands in line at Starbucks, too.) But cruising is not just for sex; we also love to use it on straight boys to keep them on their guard. Boo!

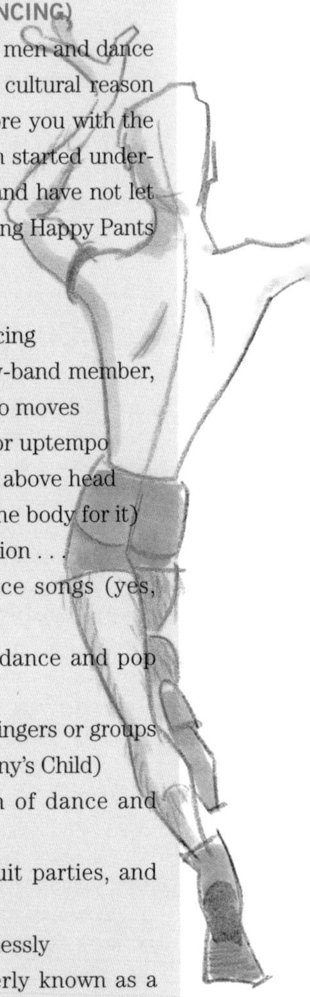

DANCE FLOOR DANDY (DANCING)

The strongest bond links gay men and dance music. There is a significant cultural reason why this is so, but I won't bore you with the details. Let's just say we both started underground, came out together, and have not let go of each other since. Spotting Happy Pants on the hardwood:

- "bops" in place before dancing
- dances *too* well, like a boy-band member, and knows all the latest video moves
- just as good dancing slow or uptempo
- high kicks and waves arms above head
- dances shirtless (but has the body for it)
- frequent chanting, in addition . . .
- knows the words to dance songs (yes, they have words!)
- knows all the latest top dance and pop tunes, but is . . .
- especially fond of female singers or groups (from the Supremes to Destiny's Child)
- has enormous collection of dance and *import* CDs at home
- talks of tea dances, circuit parties, and after-hours clubs
- sweats effusively but odorlessly
- takes a "gay nap" (formerly known as a disco nap) before going out at night—a *gaydar* classic

. . . 'TIL HE DROPS (SHOPPING)

Is there possibly anything a gay man can do better than shop?! Unlikely. If it were an Olympic event—and with all that running around, stretching, and grabbing, *why* not?—we'd win every medal (just like all those darling Eastern Bloc females used to do in swimming!). Why are we so taken with the experience? Is it the emotion, intellect, and insights we gain? Honestly, *daffodil,* it comes down to this: shopping is the easiest way to show people—especially other gay men, friends, and potential mates—that we have:

good taste (at least the kind you can buy)
a working credit/debit card (but not *always* a full bank account)
a really cute butt (do we *ever* stop?!)

Could a gay man ask for more?! Well, you do get all those goodies to sort and file when you finally arrive home! If you're interested in figuring out the gay from the straight shopper—as if I have to ask!—there are a few easy ways to do so. A first question: Is he carrying a shopping bag? If he is, the rest drops into place. Is it:

carried over his forearm, like Queen Elizabeth's handbag?
accompanied by too many more to count?
from a designer boutique, and beautifully constructed?
featuring a photo of a near-naked, humpy college boy?
shown logo(s) outward for optimum viewing by onlookers?

Answering yes to any of the above should clear away any doubts. There is also one *gaydar* classic way to tell if it is a gay man shopping:

either of two men together in a gourmet food shop

Spotted!

Gay shoppers tend to congregate in the same fashionable areas (Rodeo Drive, Michigan Avenue, Madison Avenue) and shopping establishments. (Rather startlingly for the unprepared, many of these places during peak sale periods resemble gay bars. Too bad they don't serve cocktails—that inventory could really move!) Here are some notoriously "gay" stores located near you:

Armani Exchange • D&G
Prada • Gucci • Burberry
Banana Republic • J. Crew
Abercrombie & Fitch
Restoration Hardware
Crate & Barrel
Barneys • Bloomingdale's
Saks Fifth Avenue • Neiman Marcus
Target • Home Depot • IKEA
Bed, Bath & Beyond

(Note: The above *can* change without notice. Also, cities across the country have single stores—like Bergdorf's in New York City and Maxfield's in Los Angeles—who count a sizable number of gay men among their *clientele*. Since space is limited, use the previous questionnaire to find out where the right places to shop are in town.)

Shopper's Alert!

If we do not watch our steps, shopping can quickly run us smack into that most dreaded and dreadful of homo-creations:

the conspicuous gay consumer

Fortunately, his *arriviste* obviousness makes him someone easy for your *gaydar* to find (and avoid). This man is everywhere you would expect him to be. Buying, owning, and *living* everything that is the latest, greatest, and costliest he can (and often cannot) afford. Some of us certainly have arrived, haven't we? But where, no one seems to know. However, if you did want to find out about "hip" breath fresheners and "hot" coffee bars, the bag *everyone* is carrying and the suit everyone must wear, Mr "CGC" will always have an answer. Which is typically *parvenu* of him for the course.

(Note: To be fair, it's not all his fault. Because many of us are in *these* businesses, we understandably want to keep the money in the "family." Unfortunately, cyclical thinking and the disposable income we all *supposedly* possess have created a lot of spinning spenders. Gay men caught on this "Mary"-go-round are in for a dizzying ride.

HANDY MAN (CRAFTING)

If a gay man lacks the hardwiring for hardware, the automatic skills for auto mechanics, or the spark to be an electrician, he will usually make up for it with his craftiness (and we can be *so* crafty). Starting with simple button sewing, through découpage, marbleizing, and gold leafing, his Martha Stewart-ability is always on display—and rarely goes without raves. Gift wrapping is high on his list of "can-do's" and showing off the results gives him as much pleasure as decorating cakes or making dioramas. Here are a few Hallmark ways a gay man can transform his Target purchase into your Tiffany gift:

- ***unusual-shaped boxes*** - which defy papering (triangles, cylinders) but are still skillfully covered and beribboned.
- ***the minimal use of tape*** - often hidden from view, resulting in that awed "how'd he do that?" look.
- ***coordinated wrapping*** - thematically, colorwise, and often matching the decor of the host's home.
- ***froufroued and fancifully bowed*** - but only with rayon, satin, or wired ribbon if you want to make the just-right impression with guests, receivers, and passersby.

GATHER YE ROSEBUDS (COLLECTING)

One of the things gay men have is an ability to keep an appreciation of the past alive—and *still* head toward the future. We collect even the most trivial item (or information) and store it away—in our hearts and minds, *and* in our closets and shelves!—as gentle but tangible reminders that where we are will always be linked to where we've been. And to know that one day, while an old copy of *Flair* magazine, a Maria Montez glossy, a Connie Francis 45, or a Stork Club ashtray may not bring us untold riches, it will bring inspiration and a smile—even if it is just our own—and a thank you for having the gay foresight to rescue it from oblivion.

SET IT DOWN, ALREADY (FUTZING)

In the tradition of Neil Simon's *The Odd Couple* (that was a story about gay men, wasn't it?!) a messy person can be offset with a neat person—to great comic effect. However, it's a very serious matter if the former lives with the latter, and the meals are cooked, the house is clean, and the bills are paid. If this is the case, Mr "Gets-by-on-His-Looks-and-Wits" (or so he thinks) should count his blessings. Unless, of course, his "Mr Cook-Clean-and-Organize" also turns out to be "the nervous nelly who could leave nothing alone." This obsessive-compulsive futzer can be one mean "queen" bee, as he endlessly buzzes around his hive, picking up pollen and depositing it in its proper place. Stop him and you could get stung. Nor does this hovering stay within his own home: he will dart around his desk at work, meddle in his mother's things, fidget at a friend's flat, and land just long enough to straighten the racks in Saks, before he's back home ready to move everything around again.

GAYS ON THE GO (TRAVELING)

Something about travel is most enticing to gay men. Is it the extravagance of it? Even among our child-free circles, we don't all have the money or time. This makes travel still a luxury—and we do like *luxe* things. Or is it the mind-broadening experience of seeing indigenous peoples on their native soils and unspoiled acreage in the wilderness? Yeah, right! Where's the mall?! As long as it takes us away from here (first or at least business class, please)—even if it's just for a three-day weekend excursion (a very common gay thing to do)—we were born to roam. Gay travel also happens to be a great way to:

- keep abreast of the latest trends (they don't all come from New York, *sugarplum*)
- supply us with droll conversation droppers like "London was rainy, but lovely as ever" or "Paris? Not in the summer!"
- meet men (as if it was necessary to fly or drive anywhere for us to do that!)
- show off designer, roll-away luggage
- accumulate frequent flier miles, so we can travel even more
- discover new places to go and stay which we can then recommend to family, friends, and strangers

Where the Boyz Go

It's not true that gay men only like to travel to places where they can get lattes-to-go and custom-fitted loafers. Every once in a while, you'll find us in places that haven't even heard of Gucci. But let's be realistic, most of us—if we don't already live there—will choose one of these gay culture capitals as our ultimate destination:

Paris • London
Berlin • Amsterdam
San Francisco • Los Angeles
New York City • Venice
Sydney • Barcelona
Vienna • Rome

We also travel together (and separate) in combinations rarely seen with straight men—*en masse* (like a pack of hungry wolves, actually); with a choice selection of friends; as a couple (romantically and/or platonically); or solo—because our freewheeling lifestyles allow it. And will stay (if not at the Four Seasons or a trendy boutique hotel) in the protective environment of a guest house, bed & breakfast, or "exclusive" resort—accommodations *too* close for comfort for most traveling straight men.

UNTIL GOLDEN BROWN (TANNING)

Travel may be its own reward, but getting a tan is a bonus most gay men can't do without. We have even developed a regimen guaranteed to get results. Whole groups of gay men will turn their bodies over at precise fifteen-minute or half-hour intervals, in order to ensure even coloring from front to back. In addition, seating arrangements shift with the constant movement of the sun—*our friend!*—so that no potential shadow will alter coloration from head to foot. Gay men will also have with them varying SPF lotions, which he edits away as the depth of his tan shields him from harmful UV rays.

Why is a tan so coveted? Well, all-over ones have the look of hedonistic indulgence (grrrr!), and tan-lines—which are usually called a "Speedo"—make a guy's natural *ass*ets look just like a target (bull's-eye!). Not surprisingly, many women dislike these looks quite intensely (hence, why most straight men stay away from them and end up walking off the beach with a dreaded "redneck" or "farmer's tan") but they are something that many gay men salivate over—and for the most flagrantly lascivious reasons. Naughty, naughty boys! (Note: Lucky gay European men never run into this darkening dilemma. For them, it's allowable to go without or wear a "suit" no bigger than a coin purse on a cord. Okay, for some of these men covering up their "coin roll" would take a *really* big money sack. Zowee!

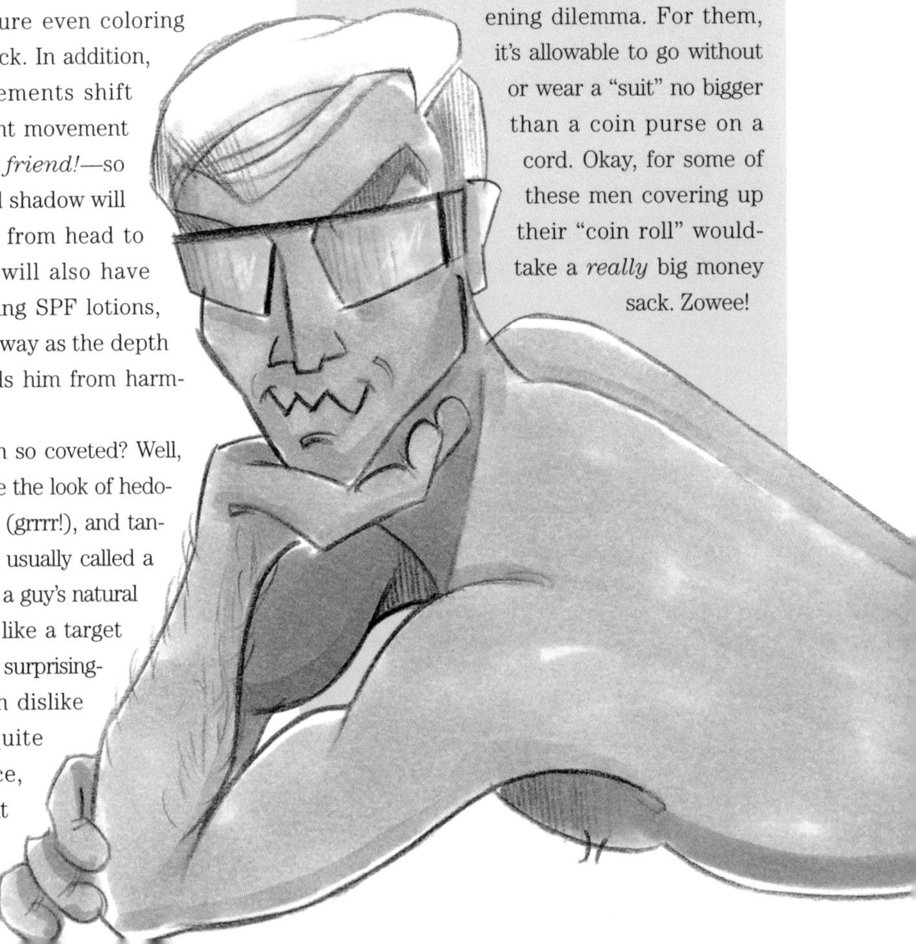

Where the Boyz Go, Too

To cultivate his tan, here are few places where Mr Sandman or pool boy can be found having fun under the sun:

South Beach, Miami, Florida
Palm Springs, California
Key West, Florida
Fire Island, New York
Provincetown, Massachusetts
Ft. Lauderdale, Florida
Rehoboth Beach, Delaware
Saugatuck, Michigan
Pensacola, Florida
Ogunquit, Maine
Mykonos, Greece
Sydney, Australia
Côte d'Azur, France
Ibiza, Spain
Rio de Janeiro, Brazil

Gay Travel Fears

- You will see him asleep on an airplane, with his mouth open and drooling. (Eek!)
- His rent-a-car will be an ugly color (white, evergreen, tan). (Yuck!)
- He will be spotted by first-class friends while seated in economy. (Gads!)
- No one will notice that he's been gone or, worse, care where he's been. (Nooooo!)
- It will be rainy, so he can't work on his tan. (*Merde!*)
- The best night to go out is the evening before or after he has arrived in town. (Phooey!)
- Arriving in a gay-friendly resort town during a "lesbian" or "straight" party weekend. (Yeeks!)
- The exchange rate is *not* in his favor. (Drat!)

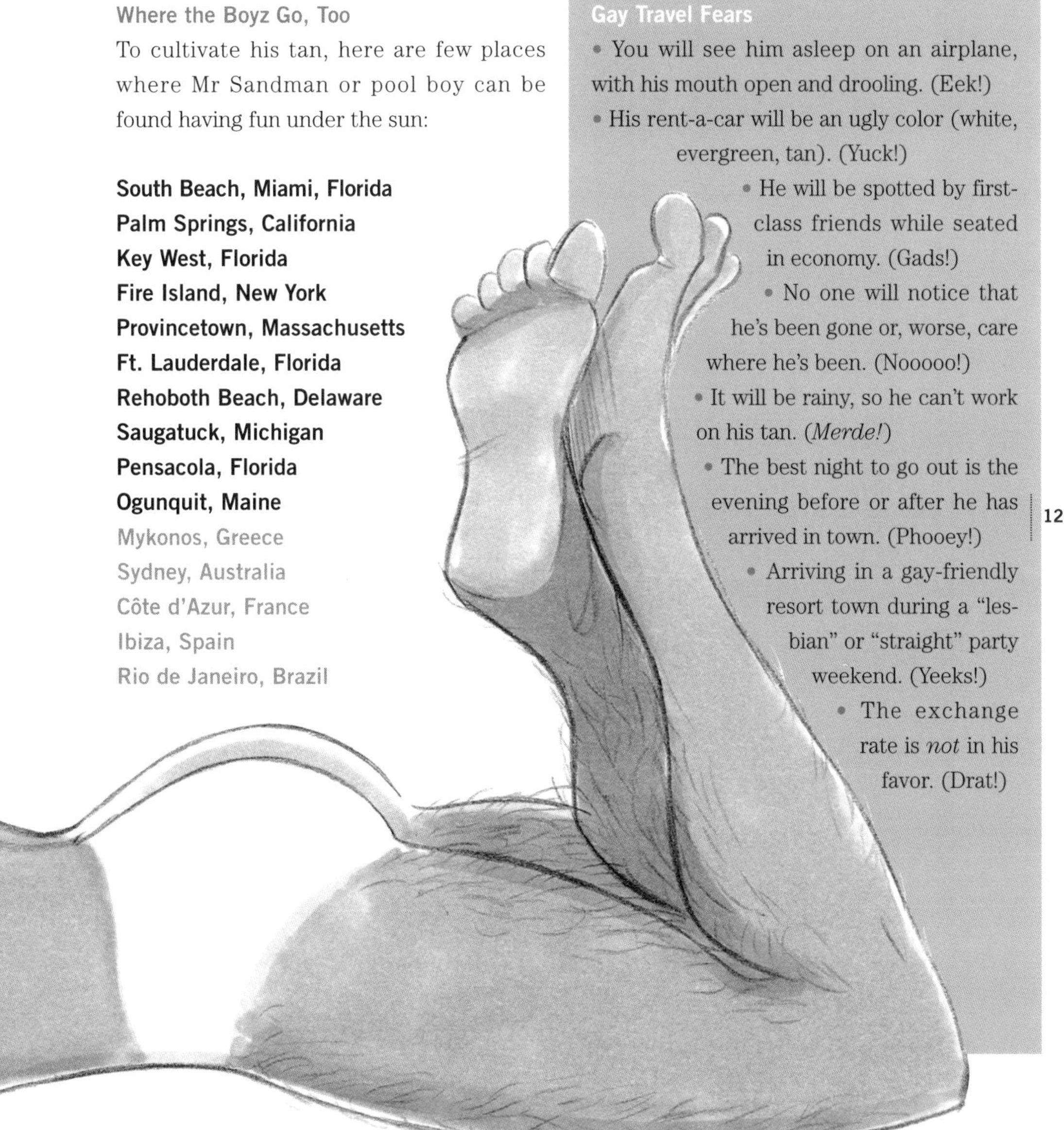

THE SHOW MUST GO ON! (VIEWING)

Our "gay" relationship with Hollywood—and the entire world of entertainment—has been long and *fruitful*. So it is with little hesitation that I offer this statement: no actor or actress, film, show, play, or recording worth the muster can afford to escape our detection if ascending to the highest heights of success is an objective. Nevertheless, this brazen affrontery—which is shared with most of my "brothers"—has spawned two long-lasting misconceptions: everyone in Hollywood is gay *and* that the town would be nothing without us. If these were true, how do you explain Arnold Schwarzenegger and Sylvester Stallone? (Hmmm, gay men do have an answer for that one.) Yes, the affair between us and Hollywood is deep, but how so remains an open issue. Regardless, the ties are so innumerable it was necessary to select specific categories and compile lists. Besides, it's a little neater this way, too. All gay men will agree with some of the final choices, and some gay men will agree with them all, but as is always the way with us, all of us could never agree on all of them, and hence, multiple debates should ensue.

10 gay-fave female film stars

This random order listing does not include "singing" stars or "current" acting faves.

- Bette Davis
- Joan Crawford
- Elizabeth Taylor
- Marlene Dietrich
- Grace Kelly
- Marilyn Monroe
- Katharine Hepburn
- Sophia Loren
- Greta Garbo
- Audrey Hepburn

10 gay-fave female "camp" stars

- Maria Montez
- Zsa Zsa Gabor
- Doris Day
- Mamie Van Doren
- Mae West
- Jayne Mansfield
- Tallulah Bankhead
- Carmen Miranda
- Hattie McDaniel
- Divine (Harris Glenn Milstead)

Now Why Didn't *We* Think of That?

In theatres, some "straight" men skip seats in between to discourage "gay" suspicions? What happens if the movie is sold out?

5 gay-fave male film stars (and a film)

Followed by five (plus one) up-and-comers whose status we will check in a few years.

- Tom Cruise (*Risky Business,* 1983)
- Brad Pitt (*Thelma and Louise,* 1991)
- Rock Hudson (*Pillow Talk,* 1959)
- Montgomery Clift (*The Heiress,* 1949)
- Paul Newman (*Sweet Bird of Youth,* 1962)
- Hugh Jackman
- Owen Wilson (and/or brother Luke)
- Tobey Maguire
- Thomas Jane
- Taye Diggs

15 gay-fave movies

- *All About Eve* (1950)
- *Auntie Mame* (1958)
- *What Ever Happened to Baby Jane?* (1962)
- *Valley of the Dolls* (1967)
- *The Wizard of Oz* (1939)
- *Breakfast at Tiffany's* (1961)
- *The Women* (1939)
- *Imitation of Life* (1959)
- *Mildred Pierce* (1945)
- *Mommie Dearest* (1981)
- *The Birds* (1963)
- *Sunset Boulevard* (1950)
- *A Star Is Born* (1954)
- *Mahogany* (1976)
- *Airport* (1970)

5 important gay-themed movies

- *The Boys in the Band* (1970)
- *Another Country* (1984)
- *My Beautiful Laundrette* (1985)
- *Longtime Companion* (1987)
- *La Cage aux Folles* (1978)

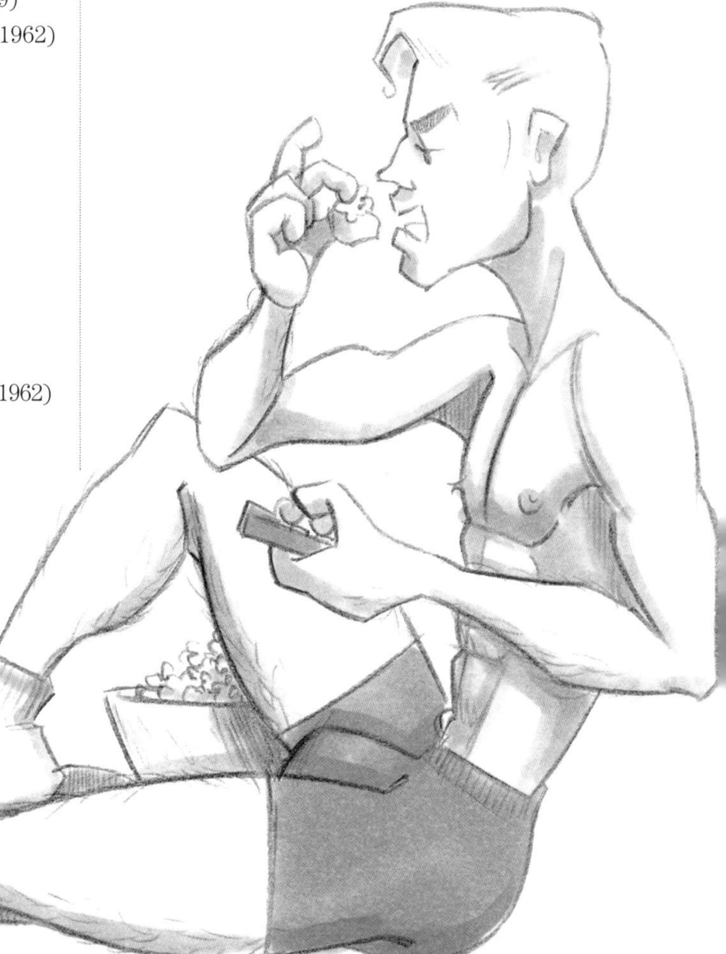

Television has given gay men much to be thankful for, including a host of stars, vehicles, and characters to adore and emulate:

5 gay-fave female television stars

- Lucille Ball
- Betty White
- Carol Burnett
- Mary Tyler Moore
- Beatrice Arthur

10 gay-fave female TV characters (past and present)

- Mary Richards (Mary Tyler Moore, *The Mary Tyler Moore Show*)

- Blanche Devereaux (Rue McClanahan, *The Golden Girls*)
- Samantha Stephens (Elizabeth Montgomery, *Bewitched*)
- Samantha Jones (Kim Cattrall, *Sex and the City*)
- Sandra Clark (Jackee Harry, *227*)
- Ginger Grant (Tina Louise, *Gilligan's Island*)
- Alexis Carrington (Joan Collins, *Dynasty*)
- Karen Walker (Megan Mullally, *Will & Grace*)
- Florence Jean ("Flo") Castleberry (Polly Holliday, *Alice*)
- Suzanne Sugarbaker (Delta Burke, *Designing Women*)

5 gay-fave television shows

- *Sex and the City* (1998–present)
- *Absolutely Fabulous* (1992–96, 2001)
- *The Mary Tyler Moore Show* (1970–77)
- *Bewitched* (1964–73)
- *The Golden Girls* (1985–92)

5 "should be gay" male TV characters

- Uncle Arthur (Paul Lynde, *Bewitched*)
- Felix Unger (Tony Randall, *The Odd Couple*)
- Niles Crane (David Hyde Pierce, *Frasier*)
- Chandler Bing (Matthew Perry, *Friends*)
- Mr French (Sebastian Cabot, *Family Affair*)

And just for the hell of it:

5 "must be gay" animated characters

- Bugs Bunny (and/or Daffy Duck)
- Flower (*Bambi*)
- Bobby Hill (*King of the Hill*)
- Hermie (*Rudolph, the Red-Nosed Reindeer*)
- Milhouse van Houten (*The Simpsons*)

5 "scenes" that have made gay men cry

- "No place like home" (*The Wizard of Oz*)
- "Misfit Island campfire" (*Rudolph*)
- "Looking for Cat" (*Breakfast at Tiffany's*)
- "Good-bye, Momma" (*Imitation of Life*)
- "Wind Beneath My Wings" (Bette Midler, *The Tonight Show with Johnny Carson*, final telecast)

The music "diva" plays an especially vital role in gay male culture. The reason: these women often sing about relationships with men (the cads!) in heartbreaking or empowering terms. Could there be a better match?

10 gay-fave divas

- Donna Summer
- Bette Midler
- Aretha Franklin
- Whitney Houston
- Eartha Kitt
- Maria Callas
- Sarah Vaughan
- Peggy Lee
- Grace Jones
- Madonna

5 divine "diva" moments

- "And I Am Telling You I'm Not Going" (Jennifer Holliday, from the Broadway show *Dreamgirls*)
- "Rose's Turn" (Ethel Merman, from the original Broadway run of *Gypsy*)
- "Don't Rain on My Parade" (Barbra Streisand, from the 1968 film *Funny Girl*)
- "The Man That Got Away" (Judy Garland, from the film *A Star Is Born*)
- "Nessun Dorma" (Aretha Franklin, from *The 1998 Grammy Awards Show*)

Music videos are also an important part of the gay media mix. (Where do you think we get all those groovy dance moves?) From back when they were still *relatively* new:

5 gay-fave music videos

- "Vogue" (Madonna, 1990)
- "Love Shack" (The B-52s, 1989)
- "Everybody, Everybody" (Black Box, 1990)
- "Free Your Mind" (En Vogue, 1992)
- "Groove Is in the Heart" (Deee-Lite, 1990)

10 gay-fave "Gay White Way" musicals

Is it every gay man's wish to see at least one actual Broadway musical? Maybe. It may all depend on how "your" list matches this one.

- *My Fair Lady*
- *Chicago*
- *A Chorus Line*
- *Dreamgirls*
- *Hello, Dolly!*
- *Follies*
- *Sweet Charity*
- *Gypsy*
- *Evita*
- *Carrie, the Musical*(!)

Gay-fave entertainment hall-of-famers

And you thought I forgot them, didn't you?!

- Judy Garland
- Liza Minnelli
- Cher
- Barbra Streisand
- Diana Ross

gaycheck

You've done it! You finished reading *Gaydar* (you did read it all, didn't you?) and are ready and anxious to play Dr Kinsey, right? I expected as much. Just remember, even he knew the answers he got weren't always truthful ones. So be wise and wary when using this questionnaire (and use a pencil or make copies; I don't think you'll be doing this once).

How to Score (*Gaydar*-wise, boys!)

Pick only one response from either the left (one point) or right (two point) side. When all have been asked, tally points to determine final placement:

0 – definitely living in Kansas
1 to 25 – leaving Kansas
26 to 50 – sees the rainbow
51 to 75 – on the rainbow
76 to 99 – over the rainbow
100 – definitely lives in Oz

1)	Does he "snigger," "giggle," or "guffaw"?	☐	While laughing, does he ever use the demure "hide-the-teeth" gesture?	☐
2)	Does he ever "squeal," go "awww," or "ewww?"	☐	Does he hate bugs and going barefoot, but love card stores and cuddly toys ?	☐
3)	Can he use a "gay" word without any painful effort?	☐	Has he ever quoted a line used in "Quotable Queer?"	☐
4)	Has he ever "gay-ified" a name?	☐	Has he ever described someone as a "drama queen" or "theatre queen"?	☐
5)	Does he ever use bits of foreign tongues when he speaks?	☐	Does he ever talk French on his cell phone?	☐
6)	Does he behave like the "gay" sensation, sweetheart, sissy, or snoot?	☐	Does he ever "strike a pose" for real or imaginary cameras?	☐
7)	Does he sit in one of the "gay" positions?	☐	Does his shoe ever hang off the foot in a "toe dangler"?	☐
8)	Is he an *out*-standing stander?	☐	When bending over, does he ever throw one "leg up"?	☐
9)	Does he walk a "gay" walk?	☐	Has he ever pranced over a puddle?	☐

10)	Does he roll his eyes when he talks?	☐	Does he arch his brows or flail his hands when he talks?	☐
11)	Have you ever caught him doing one of the "gay" stares?	☐	Can he make the "evil eye"?	☐
12)	Has he ever held a "gay" job or have friends in "the business"?	☐	Has he held more than one "gay" job?	☐
13)	Is his home decorated in one of the "gay" modes?	☐	Does he live in a "gay" neighborhood?	☐
14)	Does he use any of the signature eight "gay" decor items?	☐	More than one item?	☐
15)	Does any part of the walking tour sound like his home?	☐	Does he redecorate for holiday or special occasions?	☐
16)	Does he own a small or "toy" dog?	☐	Does he own a cat?	☐
17)	Does he have a great body?	☐	Is he post-thirty with a great body?	☐
18)	Manicured hands?	☐	Pedicured feet?	☐
19)	Does he (or did he ever) have a goatee?	☐	Does he shave off the hair on these parts of his body: the underarms, legs, or groin?	☐
20)	Does he spend extra time on his face?	☐	Is he a brow plucker or lip swirler?	☐
21)	Is he pierced?	☐	Is the piercing a navel ring or Prince Albert?	☐
22)	Is he tattooed?	☐	Is the tattoo a sunburst, arrow, or Winnie-the-Pooh above his rear?	☐
23)	Is he very clothes conscious?	☐	Does he ever play the "label game"?	☐
24)	Could you describe his clothes with a "gay" wardrobe word?	☐	Does he have multiples of the same swimsuits or sunglasses?	☐

25)	Does he wear pastels?	☐	Does he know color legend and lore, or does he match colors?	☐
26)	Is he one of the "gay" dressers?	☐	Does he change his outfit more than twice in a day?	☐
27)	Does he own a "gay" clothing item?	☐	Does he own more than one?	☐
28)	Does he wear white, brief-cut, seamed-pouch underwear?	☐	Does he ever wear a jockstrap under his shorts?	☐
29)	Does he own a pair of fashion pants?	☐	Does he wear them with designer sandals?	☐
30)	Does he wear a good watch?	☐	Does he also wear silver chain bracelets?	☐
31)	Does he know how to tie a bow tie?	☐	Does he own sock garters?	☐
32)	Has he ever made something into a dressing "prop"?	☐	Has he ever worn his jacket as a "cape" or a "stole"?	☐
33)	Does he do gymnastics, luge, row, blade, or cycle?	☐	Does he figure skate, wrestle, bodybuild, or dive?	☐
34)	Does he gossip a little?	☐	Does he never stop talking?	☐
35)	Does he critique a little?	☐	Does he never stop criticizing?	☐
36)	Is he a restaurant and entrée recommender?	☐	Does he order salad and water and smoke in restaurants?	☐
37)	Does he like to socialize, party, and drink?	☐	Does he drink like a "sweetheart sipper" or "gyrated libator"?	☐
38)	Does he ever like to hang out and just "cruise"?	☐	Has he ever bumped into "friends" at Starbucks?	☐
39)	Does he ever dance shirtless?	☐	Does he ever take a nap before going out at night?	☐

40)	Is he an impassioned shopper?	☐	Is he a conspicuous consumer?	☐
41)	Is he good at arts and crafts?	☐	Can he wrap a gift with minimal tape?	☐
42)	Is he a collector of memorabilia items?	☐	Are these items displayed in their own shadow boxes and dioramas?	☐
43)	As far as you know, does he futz around at home?	☐	As far as you know, does he straighten racks in retail shops?	☐
44)	Does he travel a lot?	☐	Does he own designer luggage on wheels?	☐
45)	Has he been to more than one of the culture capitals?	☐	Does he travel a lot on three-day weekends (especially to the beach)?	☐
46)	Is he an unstoppable tanner?	☐	Does he frequent any of the "fun-in-the-sun" resorts?	☐
47)	Can he name-match at least five "gay-fave" female stars?	☐	Can he name-match at least five "gay-fave" movies?	☐
48)	Can he name-match at least five "gay-fave" female TV characters?	☐	Can he name-match at least five "must be gay" male TV or animated characters?	☐
49)	Can he name-match at least five "gay-fave" divas?	☐	Can he name-match at least two "diva" moments?	☐
50)	Can he name-match at least two "gay-fave" hall-of-famers?	☐	Can he name-match at least five "gay-fave" Broadway musicals?	☐

Many things once considered absolutely "gay" have been supplanted by those of younger generations. Here is a matched-up list to show some changes that time hath wrought:

show tunes > dance remixes
bronzer > tattoos
skinny mincers > well-built egotists
safe places > right addresses

the pierced ear > the Prince Albert
collectibles > status symbols
sports-challenged > challenging sports
invisibility > visibility

The answers: page 7) This "colorful" quip was spoken by actress Norma Shearer in the "gay-fave" film *The Women* (1939); 8) This quote is from *Valley of the Dolls* (1967) and is sung by Helen Lawson (Susan Hayward) in the song "I'll Plant My Own Tree"; 18) The film inferred is *The Three Faces of Eve* (1957), which won an Oscar for lead actress Joanne Woodward; also from *Valley*—and deliriously delivered by character Neely O'Hara (Patty Duke) while writhing in the gutter (they don't make 'em like they used to!); 24) The pronunciation of the word *ever* as "evuh" can be heard in the song "What a Swell Party This Is," from the frothy musical *High Society* (1956), written by legendary gay composer Cole Porter; 36) The year was 1947, and with no more war restrictions, in a cinch (at the waist) Mr Dior brought fashion back; Dovima was a famed model of the fifties and favorite of photographer Richard Avedon; 38) The group is KC and the Sunshine Band, which was one seventies male disco acts—including Sylvester—to become a favorite of gay men; 39) The diva is none other than Grace Jones; 42) Oh bird watchers!, the "Tippi" is actress Tippi Hedren, star of *The Birds,* mother of *thesp* Melanie Griffith, and mother-in-law of *hot-cha-cha* actor Antonio Banderas; 51) The gay decorator is Emory (played by Cliff Gorman), from *Boys in the Band* (1970); 56) *Rashomon* is the acclaimed 1950 Oscar-winning Japanese film by director Akira Kurosawa; the story is a tale of a murder told from multiple perspectives; 71) "Bossa nova" literally translates into "new bump." This Brazilian-based music became popular in the early sixties—Stan Getz ("Girl from Ipanema"), Eydie Gormé ("Blame It on the Bossa Nova"), as two diverse examples—and has remained a cocktail party mainstay since; 77) "Dirk Diggler" is the lead character in the recent "gay-fave" film *Boogie Nights* (1997), played by menacing Mark Wahlberg; 85) "On the bias" means to work with fabric on the diagonal, which allows for extra ease and stretch; 86) This memorable exclamation came from the mouth of actress Faye Dunaway, portraying a demented Joan Crawford in *Mommie Dearest* (1981); 96) This sentiment is expressed by the sublime Audrey Hepburn in *Breakfast at Tiffany's* (1961); *"Recherché, n'est-ce pas?"* is part of a line spoken by actress Ann Blyth (as venomous daughter Veda) in the classic film *Mildred Pierce* (1945); 110) This offensive thought is delivered by Jennifer North (poor Sharon Tate) poolside to Neely O'Hara, in *Valley*; 111) and this rather succinct line was spoken by Audrey, again in *Breakfast.*

This book was as much about spotting gay men as it was for gay men to see things in ourselves—which we may (or may not) want to change. Evidently, our many gains over the years are being undermined by the Orwellian sentiment that "we are all created equal, but some are more equal than others" and have taken other's limitations to bind our own. We are still new as a visible group, but do not need to take on old habits to be seen. Please take something more away from *Gaydar* than the ability to judge a person "gay" by his cover. Let's use the sensitivity, compassion, and creativity everyone believes we have, and put them to much better use by once and for all closing the book on hate, fear, and prejudice.